TEACHING ABOUT WORLD CULTURES

FOCUS ON DEVELOPING REGIONS

Grades 7-12

Michelle Sanborn, Rachel Roe and Heidi Hursh
with
Robert Andersen and Pam Newman

D1473285

Center for Teaching International Relations

University of Denver
Denver, Colorado 80208

Teaching Materials From CTIR Publications

CTIR activity books are written and tested by classroom teachers who have special expertise in the pertinent content areas and pedagogies. Each book contains detailed descriptions for teachers on how to present activities, and associated mastersheets for photoduplication of student exercise sheets. Teachers thus need only a single book for use with an entire classroom of students.

CTIR activity books are designed to be used as supplements to teachers' existing curricula, and to offer varied and different information, perspectives, and pedagogies than are often contained in standard curricula. Some ooks, however, offer a presentation of activities in a sequential manner, and can be used as "mini" curricula, according to teacher and school needs.

Although CTIR Publications is committed to providing balanced views in the context of its activities and books that address controversial issues, not all individuals will consider them to be comprehensively representative of all possible perspectives. We remind teachers that it is ultimately their responsibility to provide their students with a balanced array of perspectives on such issues, and to use any supplementary teaching materials that they offer in their classrooms according to the intent and spirit of the curriculum objectives of their individual school districts and communities.

The views expressed in CTIR activity books are the authors' and do not necessarily reflect those of the publisher.

Printed in the United States of America
ISBN 0-934804-41-8

TABLE OF CONTENTS

INTRODUCTION

Teaching About World Cultures: Focus on Developing Regions is designed to be used as a source of supplementary activities for courses in geography, world history, and world cultures. In response to teacher requests for high-interest materials about developing nations, this book focuses on current issues such as political repression, multinational corporations, and urbanization. Unlike much of other materials available on developing nations, the activities in this unit emphasize the personal perspective, i.e., major issues that have affected the daily lives of ordinary people.

One group of activities deals with issues in the context of developing nations in general, while other sections include specific activities on Africa, India, China, Japan (as a counterpoint), the Middle East, and Latin America. The theme of development--economic, social, and political--is explored from a variety of perspectives. Students are challenged to consider problems from different points of view, with the Western concepts of "progress" and linear economic development not the only prescription for success considered.

Many of the activities are experiential in nature--simulations, role plays, and case studies. Others challenge current stereotypes about economic development or particular societies. Most may be used separately, or incorporated into courses or curricula on individual cultures, international relations, economics, human rights, and world government. Some are geared toward the middle school student, while others, because of the vocabulary and concepts involved, are more appropriate for high school.

These activities are intended to arouse student discussion, to raise questions, and to stimulate further inquiry. Current factual information is provided where necessary, but it is assumed that students also have access to a variety of standard factual references such as those listed in the book's bibliography.

The writing team for this publication included classroom teachers, international relations scholars, and curriculum developers.

GENERAL ACTIVITIES

Title: **FUTURE BABY**

Introduction: This is a good "kick-off" activity on development. By using the analogy of an infant's development, students can understand the problems facing developing countries. The issues affecting an infant's development are often similar to the issues affecting a country's development--weakness, vulnerability, lack of skills, need for food, survival, education, and so forth.

Objectives:

To define the concept of development
To identify factors affecting development
To compare the development of an infant with that of a developing nation

Grade Level: 7-12

Time: One class period

Materials: None

Procedure:

1. Ask students what infants will need, other than diapers, in the year 1999. List the students' answers on the chalkboard using the following or similar categories.

SURVIVAL	QUALITY OF LIFE	PROTECTION	TECHNOLOGY
Food	Education	Playpen	Stroller

2. Explain to students that these are immediate needs, but as an infant grows and develops, needs change. For instance, what will the baby need in the year 2020, or when he or she is 21 years old? List student responses on the board using the same categories as above.

3. Discuss with students the differences between an infant (a developing person) and a 21-year-old (a developed person). Which category(ies) change significantly? Which stay relatively the same? How is a baby fundamentally different from an adult? How does a baby relate differently to other people than does an adult? Why? How does the developed adult have a responsibility to the developing infant? Why?

4. Have students look at the list for the needs of a developing infant and see if there are any that would be similar to a developing nation's needs. List these on the board using the above categories. Possible suggestions

might be food, education, allies, and farm equipment. "What other needs would you add?"

5. Have students look at the list for the 21-year-old and pick out the needs that would be similar to a developed nation's needs. Suggestions are food, pollution controls, weapons, strong military, industries. "What needs would you add?" Write students' answers on the board.

6. Have students name some developing nations and some developed nations and write their answers on the board. List the characteristics which distinguish a developed nation from a developing nation. In what ways do developed nations act as parents to developing nations (providing security, money)?

How does the level of development affect the degree of dependency between nations?

Do developing nations relate differently to other developing nations than to developed nations?

Do developed nations have a moral responsibility to assist developing nations? Why or why not? In what ways can developed nations benefit from promoting development in developing nations?

Is the analogy of the "Future Baby" accurate for developing countries? Is it condescending? Are all developing countries "babies?" How might developing countries react to the analogy?

Follow-up:

1. Have students research foreign policy in their country to check if the "Future Baby" analogy is accurate.

2. Have students write and discuss their own analogies about developing and developed nations.

Title: **AIR-INDIA**

Introduction: This activity examines perceptions that lesser-developed countries sometimes have about developed countries, especially the United States. When students understand the (mis)perceptions other nations have about the United States they are that much closer to understanding the developing world. After being on the receiving end of "unfair" stereotyping, students are less likely to stereotype other nations.

Objectives:

To interpret symbols in advertisements
To identify stereotypes of Americans in an advertisement directed toward
  Asians
To recognize American stereotypes of other nations

Grade Level: 7-12

Time: One class period

Materials: Colored markers
             Large sheets of paper
             Handout #1, "Air-India"
             Handout #2, "Northwest Orient"

Procedure:

1. Divide students into groups of three or four and distribute paper and markers. Have students draw advertisements designed to attract Asians to visit the United States. After they are through, discuss what was used to lure people to the United States. What are the predominant symbols?

2. Distribute Handout #1 and discuss the ad with students using the following questions:

   What is the predominant symbol? What does it say about the United States?

   Read the copy aloud. Does it say anything about the United States being "big?" What does this word imply about the United States?

   Does the word "big" fit all of the U.S.? What does big imply about a society? Is this a negative or positive image?

   Why do you think people in India have this perception of the U.S.?

7   © CTIR
                               University of Denver

Why would advertising executives think this ad would work to get Asians to come to the U.S.?

3. Discuss with students what they think of when they talk about Japan. List the responses on the board. "Why do you have these stereotypes?" "Where did you get them?"

4. Distribute Handout #2. Discuss the ad with students.

   What is the predominant symbol in this ad? (Mount Fuji)

   Does this ad presume that Japan is the only nation United States' citizens should visit in the Orient?

   Does the copy fit the symbolism?

   Do you think the Japanese would want this picture to be the only symbol of Japan? Why or why not?

   Do you think this ad would lure U.S. citizens to the Orient? Why?

5. Discuss the similarities of the two ads with students. How are they different? Is one of them less "stereotypical" than the other? Explain. Is there a way to avoid stereotypes in advertising? How? Are stereotypes ever good? In which cases? Where do we get our impressions of other countries other than from advertising? Where do people from lesser developed countries get their images of America?

Follow-up:

1. Have students locate ads from magazines and newspapers similar to the handouts. Have students analyze the stereotypes used and how the ad limits people's perception of that country or region. Discuss the stereotypes in class and post ads in the classroom.

2. Have groups of students select different countries and have them find images in the media about that country. Decide which symbol is used most often. For example, Taj-Mahal for India and Sphinx for Egypt.

© CTIR
University of Denver

Title: **STRANDED**

Introduction: Every nation needs to develop an educational base. Educated minds help build new factories, create new works of art, and write new laws; they help develop a nation. Developing countries often do not have the resources to educate their young people, so they must send their students abroad. Many foreign students study in developed countries. They generally have different motivations and goals than students from developed countries. This activity explores the need to develop an educational base and the problems that such a need generates. It also asks the question, "Do developed countries have an obligation to educate students who come from the developing world?"

Objectives:

To justify the need for a developing country to develop an educational base along with an economic and political system
To evaluate the role of developed countries in helping to educate students from developing nations

Grade Level: 7-12

Time: One class period

Materials: Handout #3, "10,000 Nigerian Students are Stranded in U.S."

Procedure:

1. Discuss study abroad programs with students, including whether they would like to participate in such a program, and possible related problems.

   What would you like to study? Would these studies help our country? Is helping our country your primary goal in getting an education?

   If you want to study in your country, why? Could all of you study abroad if you wanted to? Why or why not?

2. Discuss study abroad programs of developing nations.

   Find out whether your students have ever met a foreign student, where they were from, and why they were here to study.

   Why do other nations send their young people to developed countries to be educated? What might a foreign student study? Why?

9

Who do you think pays for their tuition? If the person's government is paying the tuition, do they have anything to say about what the student studies?

How important do you think it is for developing countries to send their students to developed countries to study? What good do you think it would do?

Does everyone in a developing country get to be educated? Could anyone from a developing country study abroad if he/she wanted to?

3. Distribute Handout #3 and have students read it. Discuss it using the following questions as a guide.

What problems does Nigeria face? What do you think the Nigerians are studying? Can you tell from the universities mentioned in the article?

What should the U.S. government's response be? Pay for them? Let them be deported? What would that mean for Nigeria?

What are the differences between investing in the education of students from developing countries and building factories or mines in those countries? What are the benefits to your country? To the country itself?

What might some of the problems be for these students when they return to Nigeria? What problems might they have in relating to other Nigerians? How would the long exposure to Western culture affect the students' perception of their own culture?

What are some of the positives and negatives of large numbers of students from developing countries being educated in other countries?

Give some examples of other groups of students from developing countries and what their problems are and might be.

Follow-up:

1. Invite a foreign student to your class. If possible, invite students from both developing and developed nations. Compare the students' motivations and goals.

2. Contact a local university and ask for information about study abroad programs for students from your country, and about facilities at the university for foreign students.

3. Contact someone from an organization who sponsors study abroad programs and have them come to talk to the class about developed countries responsibility to educate people from developing nations.

© CTIR
University of Denver

Title: **REVOLUTION**

Introduction: This activity is an introduction to the concept of revolution--factors that contribute to this likelihood and the different ways in which it is viewed by groups within the society.

Objectives:

To evaluate the likelihood of a revolution in a particular country based on a set of criteria
To perceive different viewpoints toward a possible revolution

Grade Level:

Time: One class period and one homework assignment

Materials: Handout #4, "Criteria for Revolution"
Handout #5, "Country Cards"

Procedure:

1. Ask students to define the science of meteorology. How can a meteorologist learn to predict the occurrence of a storm? Is he/she always correct? How can forecasting be improved (e.g., better data, close observation, analysis of common occurrences before a storm, etc.)?

2. Turn the discussion to the topic of revolutions. Ask the class to list several revolutions that have occurred recently. What affect have these revolutions (e.g., East Germany, Philippines) had on your own life and on current inflation rates?

   Could anyone have predicted these revolutions? How?

   What would be the advantages of being able to predict revolutions?

   Is it as easy to predict human behavior as it is to predict the weather? What are some of the unique problems?

   Explain that the class will be experimenting with a system to predict a revolution in a particular country. Through this activity, they should be better able to understand the revolutions of the past as well as those going on today and in the future.

3. Use Handout #4 as a transparency, or list the criteria on the chalkboard. Discuss with the class the reasons why each of the conditions listed in the criteria would increase the possibility of revolution.

Ask for examples of revolutions in which these criteria may be found. Caution the students that each of the criteria is not equally weighted in a particular country, and that the <u>interaction</u> of forces inside and outside the country, as well as differing <u>perceptions</u>, will determine whether or not a revolution actually occurs.

Students may have additional suggestions to add to the list of criteria before they go on to the next part of the activity.

4. Divide the class into groups of three to four students. Give each group one of the country cards (Handout #5). Its task is to decide whether or not its country will experience a revolution in the next few years. The group should be prepared to justify its decision based on the criteria. Emphasize that it is less important to get the "right" answer than it is to <u>support</u> their decision persuasively by using the criteria.

5. Each group will give a brief report to the class, summarizing the most important facts about its country, stating its decision, and justifying it according to the criteria.

6. Ask the students if they recognize any of the countries. Then tell them what actually happened or is happening in each country based on the Teacher Notes. Discuss reasons why the class's decisions may have differed from the actual result.

7. Assign each student in the small groups a role. (Roles are listed on the bottom of each country card.) Ask him/her to write a brief description of the <u>perspective</u> of that person toward a possible revolution in their country. Descriptions should include:

a) Whether or not that person would be likely to support a revolution.

b) Specific reasons for his/her decision based on the information from the country card and the role.

c) Alliances or coalitions that this person might make with other groups in the country or outside the country.

d) Possible effects a successful revolution might have on the person's daily life.

Key to Handout #5

Country A: Peru
Country B: Philippines
Country C: Singapore
Country D: The Sudan
Country E: Guatemala
Country F: Tanzania

Title: GALTUNG'S WEB*

Introduction: We all know that nations interact with each other, and that groups of people within those nations interact with each other and with groups of people in other nations. This activity illustrates how nations and groups of people within nations interact. It is based on John Galtung's theory of structural imperialism.

Galtung has divided the world into two types of nations: Center Nations which are highly developed and have the ability to act in the global arena and also exercise that ability; and Periphery Nations which are less developed and are affected by and vulnerable to Center Nations. Further, Galtung separated the societies or groups of people in each nation into classes. Center Elite are those citizens whose actions have a significant impact on a large number of people. Periphery Elite are those individuals who help run the country, including government officials, the military, and wealthy citizens. Center Commoners are the working people who can generally communicate with their nation's elite. Periphery Commoners are the working people who are isolated from their nation's elite.

Objectives:

To become familiar with the theory of Galtung's web
To illustrate potential cultural conflict

Grade Level: 9-12

Time: One class period

Materials: Masking tape
              Handout #6, "Roles"
              Nametags in two colors
              Three colors of string or yarn
              Handout #7, "Galtung's Web: True-False Test"

Procedure:

1. Using masking tape, make twelve large circles on the floor. (See diagram on page 16.) Label each circle with the names shown on the diagram.

2. Distribute Handout #6 and have students choose which role they would like to play. Have students make a nametag for their role. Use a different color nametag for the elites and the commoners.

---

*John Galtung. Development and Technology: Toward a Technology for Self-Defense (NY: United Nations, 1979.)

3. Have students position themselves in the circles according to the diagram. Depending on how many students are in the class, either increase or decrease the number of commoners.

4. Discuss the definitions outlined in the Introduction with students. Illustrate by telling those who fit the definition to raise their hands. Take time to discuss how the students themselves fit into the definition. For the most part, young people from the United States are Center Commoners. Discuss how their parents fit the definitions. Once students understand the definitions, discuss which role would interact with another and which would not. For example, the Canadian network reporter would conceivably interview the Nigerian President, but an Indian beggar would have nothing to do with a Romanian taxi driver.

5. Go to each student and have him or her choose aloud other individuals with whom he/she would interact. If a pairing is plausible, give the two students involved one piece of string to hold between them. Use the three different colors of string to signify the type of pairing: elite-elite, elite-commoner, or commoner-commoner. If a pairing is unlikely, explain why the interaction is not likely to happen. In general, most of the elites in both center and periphery nations will be linked together, particularly center-center elites. None of the commoners will link with other commoners outside their countries. When the last student is done, the class will have formed Galtung's Web.

6. While students are still forming the web, hold a class discussion. Who is holding the most amount of strings? Who is holding the least amount? What types of people are connected? What types of nations are connected?

   Are there any elites who would have interaction with periphery commoners? In what capacity? What problems would periphery commoners have in interacting with elites of their own nations? Of other nations?

   Why would the elite of a periphery nation only speak with the elite of a center nation (as opposed to center commoners)? What does this imply?

   Are there more strings held between center elites and center commoners than between periphery elites and periphery commoners? Are there more strings held between center elites and periphery elites than between periphery elites and periphery commoners? What problems does this present for development of periphery nations?

   Would center commoners have any interactions with periphery commoners? What does this mean for possible center nation support, i.e., foreign aid, for periphery commoners? In other words, does American Farmer Brown care about the Brazilian bus driver?

   Discuss exceptions to Galtung's theory. Does the USSR really fit into the center elite/center commoner definitions, or is it a center nation with periphery elite/commoners? How do these definitions explain developed nations such as China? Which periphery nations resist center nations? Which periphery elites deliberately try to maintain contact with their own periphery commoners? How are these two questions related?

14

7. Have students return to their seats and distribute Handout #7. Review the definitions and use numbers 6, 10, 15, and 20 on the test to discuss the problem of class in developing nations.

Follow-up:

1. Have students brainstorm a list of possible interactions between center and periphery commoners.

2. Have students collect news articles about foreign affairs and then categorize these interactions according to the definitions. Do these interactions generally fit the theory?

Answers to True-False Text:

1. True	6. True	11. True	16. True
2. True	7. True	12. True	17. True
3. False	8. False	13. False	18. False
4. True	9. True	14. True	19. True
5. False	10. True	15. True	20. True

© CTIR
University of Denver

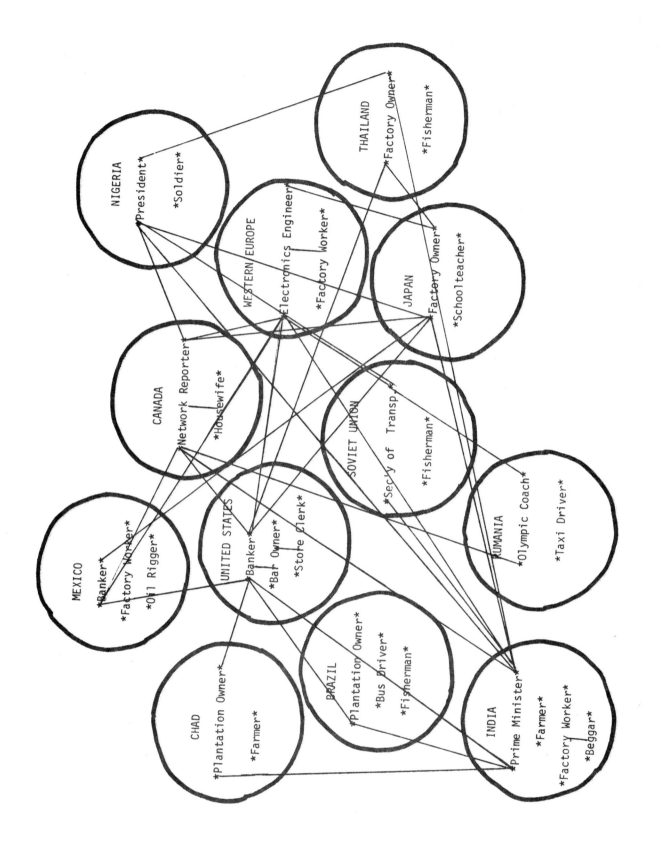

16

CHINA ACTIVITIES

Title: **PAPERCUTS: REFLECTIONS OF CHANGE**

Introduction: Papercuts, one of China's oldest traditional folk arts, are thought to have originated as early as the sixth century. Still very popular, the designs serve as a graphic indication of changes in Chinese culture. During the Cultural Revolution (1966-1976) they took on a very political tone, but have now returned to some of the traditional themes. This activity introduces students to papercuts as an art form. It encourages them to think about how art reflects changes in culture. Designs and instructions are also provided if students wish to make their own.

Objectives:

To examine Chinese papercuts as a unique form of folk art
To analyze a set of papercuts for evidence of cultural change in China
To create papercuts using authentic designs

Grade Level: 5-12

Time: One to two class periods

Materials: Handout #8, "Designs" (One set mounted or laminated for display
             and one set for each group of students)
         Handout #9, "Papercuts Information Sheet"
         Assorted papercuts (OPTIONAL), available from oriental art stores,
             bookstores, or make your own. Books with designs may be
             purchased through:
                        China Books and Periodicals
                        2929 24th Street
                        San Francisco, CA 94110
                        415/282-2994
         Exacto knives or small scissors
         Carbon paper
         Cardboard or other cutting surface

Procedure:

1. Display papercuts (Handout #8) around the room and ask students to examine them.

    How do you think the designs are made?

    What are they used for?

    What country are they from? Why do you think so?

19   © CTIR
                                   University of Denver

Discuss student responses and, depending on the grade level of the students, explain some of the material found in the Teacher Background information.

2. Using overhead transparencies or photocopies of the papercut designs, classify the designs as traditional or modern. This may be done by the class as a whole, in small groups, or as individuals. There will probably be some discrepancies in classification, which can lead to a discussion of what is meant by the terms traditional and modern and how many things in developing countries are a mixture of the two.

3. Distribute Handout #8. Have students individually, or in small groups complete and make conclusions about evidence of cultural change.

4. Discuss student responses to the handout, making use of the notes on specific papercuts as needed. Dates refer to when the papercuts were purchased in China, or if they are traditional designs, that occur frequently in pre-1949 art. Refer to key below for description of each papercut.

(1) Double Happiness pattern--Traditional design found in various forms throughout Chinese art.
(2) Children participating in political action campaign, possibly traffic safety--1980, illustrates use of papercuts for political education.
(3) Butterfly and flowers--1980.
(4) Latin American Revolutionary--1973, during the Cultural Revolution China actively backed revolutionary groups in Latin America and much propaganda was directed against "American imperialism" in the Third World.
(5) Woman welder--1973, women are becoming more common in heavy industry in China, working as welders, or construction crane operators.
(6) Horses in circle--Found in an archaeological excavation dating from the sixth century B.C.; discovered in 1959 in Northwest China.
(7) Peasant, worker, and PLA soldier--1973, these were the three model citizens of the Cultural Revolution, when solidarity between workers, peasants, and the army was emphasized.
(8) Mao Zedong--1973, although Mao is still considered a great revolutionary leader, he is not the object of a cult as he was during the Cultural Revolution.
(9) Dragon--1980, dragons were considered symbols of imperial decadence during the Cultural Revolution; they have begun to appear in Chinese art again.
(10) Minority woman feeding pig--1980, official government policy is to encourage preservation of minority languages and culture.
(11) Minority children with musical instruments--1980, a common form of entertainment in Chinese schools is learning songs and dances from the minorities, just as American students learn about American Indians.
(12) Black man--1973, during the Cultural Revolution, Chinese students were taught about racism in the United States as a means of discrediting the American system.

(13) Plum Blossom--Traditional pattern, symbol of winter.
(14) Shou--Traditional symbol of longevity.
(15) Ts'ai Shen--Traditional god of wealth.

Follow-up: Use Handout #8 designs as models for students to create their own papercuts. Modify the following directions for younger students.

Distribute supplies. The best kind of paper to use is what art stores call "fadeless," a thin stiff paper colored on one side. Origami paper also works well, but is smaller and somewhat more expensive. Exacto knives may be shared by two or three students. To make inexpensive knives, cut short pieces off an old clock spring. Mount between strips of bamboo or pliant wood and bind securely with wire or glue. Sharpen to a pointed blade. Students will also need carbon paper and a piece of cardboard to use as a cutting board. Use the carbon paper to trace the design. Cut out carefully. Papercuts may be mounted on oiled paper and put on a window to be especially authentic. (See Teacher Background.)

Teacher Background: The papercut is one of China's oldest forms of folk art. Archaeologists have found samples that date back to the early sixth century A.D., several hundred years after the invention of paper in China. Papercuts are called "window flowers" in China because they were traditionally used as window decorations for the New Year, or Spring Festival. To prepare for the New Year, families cleaned, swept, and put their houses in order. New paper, made partially transparent by applying tung oil, was pasted into the windows. On these fresh windows were pasted the papercuts, which made colorful decorations and symbolized joy and happiness. Other papercuts (called men-hua or door pictures) were used on the door lintels. Papercuts have also been used to decorate fans, lanterns, gifts, and mirrors, and to serve as patterns for embroidery. In modern China, they have carried political and educational messages, have been used to decorate book covers, and have served as patterns for woodcuts, shadow puppets, animated films, postage stamps, and designs on cloth. Because it is versatile and inexpensive, the papercut has remained a popular form of folk art in China.

Many of the traditional papercut designs are important folk art symbols. If students are interested in researching some of these symbols, they may refer to sources listed in Materials, as well as to general works on Chinese art. The most common colors used in papercuts were red, black, and white, although those made today are in a variety of colors. Many are made in small rural workshops, a number of copies at a time. Skilled craftsmen, using small knives, can make up to forty at a time. Styles differ throughout China, with a more delicate style predominating in the south and the northern style more forceful. For example, Papercut #3 is a good example of the southern style, and #2 is typical of the bolder style of the north.

During the Sino-Japanese War (World War II), Communists began to use papercuts for political education, displaying papercuts of militiamen and other symbols of resistance in their windows. During the Cultural Revolution (1966-1976), the use of papercuts for political purposes reached a peak. Most forms of art, including Chinese opera, novels, ballets, movies, paintings, and sculpture, were judged by their political "message" and creativity was discouraged. The papercut designs in this activity are a good example of how art was used to educate people during this period. With the death of Mao Zedong in 1976, and the change in government policy toward art in the late 1970s, papercut designs returned to some of the more traditional themes as well as reflecting the ethnic diversity of China.

© CTIR
University of Denver

Title: **MODEL STUDENT**

Introduction: The values of Chinese society today are reflected in its educational system. In this activity, students examine a set of rules that were printed on the inside cover of a Chinese school book, compare them with their own school rules, and decide whether or not the Chinese rules would reinforce the goals of a developing nation.

Objectives:

To compare the Chinese rules with those of an American school
To analyze the Chinese rules for underlying values
To evaluate the rules in relation to the goals of a developing nation
To match the rules with the pictures on a poster from China

Grade Level: 5-12

Time: One class period

Materials: List of own school's rules (if available)
              Handout #10, "Rules for Chinese Students"
              Slides or pictures of a Chinese school (OPTIONAL)

Procedure:

1. Post or make a handout of your own school's rules or code of conduct. (If there is none, discuss why it is not in writing and compile one based on student perceptions.)

2. Divide class into pairs and distribute Handout #10. Ask students to list similarities and differences between the two sets of rules.

3. If slides or pictures of a Chinese school are available, show them at this point. Note the number of students in each classroom (usually about fifty) and the methods of instructions, physical environment, dress, and appearance of students. Relate to the rules and the preceding discussion of similarities and differences with your schools.

4. Compile a class list of similarities and differences between your schools and Chinese schools based on what has been learned from the rules and slides.

Adapted from an activity by Patricia Fernquist, CTIR, 1983. Used by permission.

Ask students to make conclusions about the differences in values between the two educational systems (e.g., the Chinese rules put great emphasis on the group).

5. In small groups, or as a class, have students make inferences about Chinese society today and its priorities based on what they know about its educational system. Identify what students believe to be the basic values of the society.

6. Discuss with students the values identified with the goals of development. Which values reflected in the rules would be especially important in a developing country?

   During which historical period(s) in the United States were these same values emphasized?

   Are there similar patterns in the needs of American society during those periods and the needs of Chinese society today (e.g., Puritan New England, Western frontier, Industrial Revolution)?

   How does an educational system reflect a nation's stage of development?

   How does an educational system fit into a nation's plans for development (skills, nationalism, values)?

   OPTIONAL: If the class has studied Chinese history--Which of the Chinese school rules are closest to the teachings of Confucius? Which represent new revolutionary values? How do you think they might change as China develops?

© CTIR
University of Denver

Title: PYRAMID POWER: CHINA'S ONE BILLION PEOPLE

Introduction: China, with over one billion people and almost one-quarter of the total world population, has embarked on an ambitious program for population control. By analyzing population pyramids for China and the United States, students will identify differences and predict possible problems for China because of the age distribution of its current population.

Objectives:

To become familiar with reasons to be able to predict future populations
To interpret and analyze data

Grade Level: 7-12

Time: One class period

Materials: Project statistics on number of students per grade in your school now and in 1990 (OPTIONAL)
Handout #11, "Population Pyramid-China"
Handout #12, "Population Pyramid-United States"
Handout #13, "Population Pyramid Questionnaire"

Procedure:

1. (OPTIONAL) As a way of introducing the activity in a meaningful way to your students, especially in districts experiencing declining enrollment and/or uneven age distributions, ask the students:

   What kinds of information would you need in order to estimate the number of students in each grade in your school in 1990 (number of children in each of the lower age groups now, rate of growth of the community due to families moving in, etc.)?

   What factors that are part of planning for the school would depend on these estimates of future population (number of teachers and classrooms needed, supplies, etc.)?

   Ask the students to estimate the number of students in each grade in 1990 and then show them the actual estimates. Discuss what changes in the school will result from changes in both the total population and the population distribution among the grades in the school.

2. Discuss the importance of being able to predict future population at particular age levels. On a national level, consumer product sales may change, retirement and Social Security demands may increase, and education may need to become more of a lifelong process.

For developing countries, the need to be able to predict changes in population age distribution is especially vital. The median age of the population in many developing countries such as China is below the age of twenty. According to the last U.S. Census, the median age in that country is now over thirty. Social scientists have termed the change from a rapidly growing population to a more stable one the "demographic transition," and have hypothesized that economic development is the major factor influencing this transition.

Depending on the age level of the students, discuss some of the ideas above, and distribute Handouts #11, #12, and #13.

3. Using Handout #11, review with students how to read a population pyramid. The first questions on Handout #13 are intended to check their ability to interpret the chart.

4. Ask students to complete Parts A, B, and C of Handout #13. You may wish to check each section before going on to the next.

5. Discuss the charts and students' answers.

The Chinese government has launched a campaign to limit families to one child. Explain why such strict population control is vital to China's development.

By referring to the Chinese population pyramid, explain why it would take at least thirty years for a population control program to be effective in stabilizing China's population growth.

How would the budget needs of a developing country with a population age distribution such as China's differ from the budget needs of a country with an age distribution like the United States?

How do you expect China's population pyramid to change by the year 2000? Sketch what you think it will look like.

Title: GRASSROOTS GOVERNMENT: THE NEIGHBORHOOD COMMITTEE

Introduction: With the decline in the role of the extended family as a form of social control in China, new institutions have developed to deal with everyday problems. One of the most effective is the neighborhood committee, (or residents' committee), the smallest unit of local government with jurisdiction over approximately 100-600 households. Functions of the neighborhood committees include public security, mediating in civil disputes, child care, public sanitation, maintaining public works, implementing government campaigns, and cultural enrichment. In this activity, students role play members of a neighborhood committee making decisions on three typical cases.

Objectives:

To identify problems that might be solved by neighborhood committees in China today
To analyze changes in forms of social control from the traditional Chinese family and clan system to the neighborhood committee
To compare this form of social control to that in your country

Grade Level: 7-12

Time: One class period

Materials: Handout #14, "Who Can I Turn To?"
Handout #15, "The Neighborhood Committee"
Handout #16, "Three Cases"

Procedure:

1. Distribute Handout #14. After each problem, ask students to list the person, group, or institution they would turn to for help in solving that problem.

2. Discuss student responses. Explain that each of these problems could be handled in China by a group called the neighborhood committee. Although in traditional China the extended family or clan made these decisions, the old authority structure has begun breaking down and new institutions are assuming the functions of social control on a local level.

3. Distribute Handout #15. Discuss the organization of the neighborhood committee. Choose a chairperson to run the meeting and serve as representative to the street committee, the next highest level of government. Distribute Handout #16 and assign roles in the three cases.

27

Give students time to discuss their roles and to plan what they will say in the meeting. <u>Note:</u> Teachers may adjust the number of roles and their descriptions to the size and level of maturity of the class.

4. Hear each case individually, allowing time for students to go through the three steps in the process as described in Handout #15. Caution them against narrowing in on one solution before exploring a variety of alternatives. Although you do not want to stifle creative problem-solving, encourage students to remain realistic and to consider the nature of Chinese society today. Hold a vote of the total class to choose the solution for each case. Insist on consensus, rather than simple majority rule.

5. After hearing all three cases and proposing solutions for each, ask students if these three cases could be interrelated. Are there ways in which individuals involved in one case could help solve another (e.g., the retired mother of eight might be able to pick up the working woman's children at the day care center)? Allow time for discussion of a variety of interrelationships. Diagram them on the board or on butcher paper, emphasizing the idea of the community as an interrelated system or a web of relationships.

6. Discuss how the Chinese neighborhood functions as an interrelated, interdependent community.

   What role does the neighborhood committee play?

   Compare the neighborhood committee with similar institutions in American culture (urban neighborhood groups, churches, etc.).

   Do other developing countries face similar social problems as a result of weakening family and tribal ties? Give examples.

   What suggestions might you make to other developing countries based on the Chinese experience? Which characteristics of the neighborhood committee in China are exportable and which are probably specific to the Chinese situation?

   How could the neighborhood committee be used by the Chinese government or by individuals in destructive ways? Was the same true of the family/clan system?

Title: HOW ARE YOU GOING TO KEEP THEM DOWN ON THE FARM?

Introduction: A typical phenomenon in a developing country is massive rural-urban migration, caused in part by economic disparities and urban cultural advantages. Some cities, such as Cairo, Egypt, Lagos, Nigeria, and Mexico City have experienced unusually rapid urban growth, causing problems with housing, sanitation, transportation, and social disintegration. China's government has recognized the serious consequences of a large influx of population into its cities and has tried a number of solutions in the past thirty years. In this activity, students use a case study and statistical data to make conclusions about the push-pull factors for the migration of Chinese peasants to the cities. Several alternative programs are presented for discouraging migration, and students are asked to choose one program and defend it. Class discussion then focuses on how these programs might be applied in other developing countries.

Objectives:

To analyze Chinese statistical and case study data for push-pull factors in
  rural-urban migration
To evaluate alternative Chinese programs to discourage migration
To apply these programs in the context of other developing countries

Grade Level: 9-12

Time: Two class periods

Materials: Handout #17, "Chinese Statistics"
              Handout #18, "Case Study"
              Handout #19, "Alternative Programs"

Procedure:

1. Distribute Handout #17. Based on the statistics, ask students to compile a list of reasons why a Chinese peasant would want to move to a city. What factors would discourage him/her from wanting to move? Discuss their answers and explain that the statistics tell only part of the story. They will now read a case study to see how these figures translate into people's daily lives.

2. Distribute Handout #18 and have students read the case study. Ask students to add additional factors to each of their lists. Discuss and then ask for a vote on whether or not they would actually try to migrate to the city if they were Mei Xiao-lan. (The class will probably vote "yes," which gives the teacher an opportunity to make the transition to the next part of the activity.)

© CTIR
                                              University of Denver

3. Discuss possible problems that might result from massive rural-urban migration (unemployment, housing shortage, poor sanitation, inadequate transportation, rise in crime). Again refer students to Handout #17 to check the unemployment rate in China. Housing is extremely limited in Chinese cities, with an average of 3.6 sq. meters per person. Pollution, traffic jams, and crime have also been on the increase. If the class has studied other cities such as Mexico City, Mexico; Calcutta, India; Cairo, Egypt; Rio de Janiero, Brazil; Lagos, Nigeria; and Tokyo, Japan, refer to them as examples of potential problems if rural-urban migration in a developing country is unchecked.

4. The Chinese government has attempted a number of solutions to the migration problem during the past thirty years. Distribute Handout #19, which describes programs the government tried at various times. Ask the students to evaluate the programs based on their own criteria and to decide which they would recommend. This may be done by individuals or in small groups. Criteria may include any or all of the following: economic development of the country, social control, individual motivation, human rights, profit, and pragmatism.

5. Discuss student choices, asking them to justify their choice of programs based on the criteria they felt were most important.

Were these criteria consistent with Chinese values today?

Are the programs workable?

What indications of success are there for any of the programs?

Will the success be maintained over a longer period of time?

How <u>will</u> China "keep them down on the farm?" <u>Should</u> they?

Does a government have the right to make such decisions based on the argument that they are avoiding the problems of a Calcutta or a Mexico City?

Follow-up: Apply the concepts in the Chinese programs to other developing countries the class has studied. Which would probably work? Which could only work in China? What recommendations would the class make to other developing countries based on the Chinese experience?

© CTIR
University of Denver

JAPAN   ACTIVITIES

Title: **JAPANESE SOCIOGRAMS**

Introduction: The family structure in Japan is different from that in the United States. In the United States, the wife and husband are generally the core of the family, but in Japan, the mother and children are an entity separate from the father. This cultural pattern creates ramifications throughout all of Japanese society, so an understanding of Japanese families is a good beginning for the exploration of Japan itself.

Objectives:

To introduce the concept of a sociogram by applying it to the student's own family
To analyze relationships within the Japanese family based on a reading
To illustrate relationships within the Japanese family by constructing a sociogram
To draw conclusions about the differences between Japanese and American families
To make hypotheses about the effects of these differences on the society at large

Grade Level: 7-12

Time: One class period

Materials: Transparency of Teacher's Family sociogram
              Handout #20, "The Japanese Family"

Procedure:

1. Using an overhead projector or the chalkboard, demonstrate to students how to draw a sociogram using your own family as the example.

2. Have students draw sociograms of their own families. Discuss the results.

    Which two individuals have the strongest line between them? Which two have the weakest line? Are there any relationships which go only one way?

    What are some factors which cause strong lines and weak lines? List these factors on the board. (Divorce, long working hours, away for college, etc.)

3. Distribute Handout #20 and read out-loud.

4. Using the reading as a guide, have students complete a Japanese family sociogram. Discuss, using the following questions as a guide.

Which individuals have the strongest link? Which individuals have the weakest? Are there any relationships which go only one way?

What does this sociogram say about the relationships within the Japanese family?

How does this sociogram compare to the one of your family?

List some differences between Japanese and American society which might be due to these familial differences.

Follow-up:

1. Make sociograms for other cultural groups.

2. Do the "Corporate Culture" activity and have a discussion about the relationship between family structure and corporate management in Japan.

3. Invite a person from Japan to your classroom to talk about the Japanese family. Then, invite a psychologist to talk about American families from your country.

4. Have a discussion about where the family is headed in your country. Are they becoming similar to Japan?

5. Have students make sociograms of extended families.

Japanese Sociogram Model

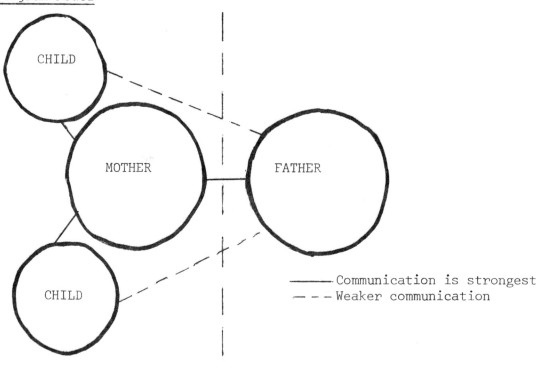

Communication is strongest
— — — Weaker communication

Title: **THE JAPANESE APARTO (HOME)**

Objectives:

To compare the concept of space in Japanese and other societies
To familiarize students with typical furniture and other articles found in a
  Japanese home
To analyze the effects of limited space on human relations

Grade Level: 7-12

Time: One class period

Materials: Handout #21, "Aparto Floor Plan"
               Handout #22, "Aparto Furnishings"
               Meter sticks
               Masking tape
               Scissors
               Large pieces of white paper

Procedure:

1. Divide the class into two groups. Group One will be responsible for
    measuring out the exact size of the Japanese aparto. Group Two will
    measure and cut out pieces of paper the size of the furniture.

2. Distribute Handout #21, the meter sticks, and the masking tape to Group
    One. Ask students to measure out the actual dimensions of the aparto and
    mark the boundaries with masking tape on the floor of the classroom.

3. Meanwhile, distribute Handout #22, scissors, and the paper to Group Two.
    Ask this group to measure and cut out pieces of paper in the shape of the
    furniture for the aparto.

4. Bring both groups back together and have them place the furnishings within
    the appropriate rooms of the aparto. This part of the activity should
    generate questions such as which room will be the bedroom or the living
    room. Will everyone sleep together in the same room? Will four futons
    fit in one room? Where do the furnishings go when they are not in use?

5. Some of the furnishings may not be used. Be sure to have students
    evaluate which items of furnishings are most important.

6. When all items are placed, have four students sit in one room of the
    aparto. Ask them the following questions:

    Do you feel crowded?

What activities do you think the Japanese do at home in the evening? How might your attitude about home be different in Japan?

7. As the four students are sitting in the apartment, have other students list possible problems they might face living in the apartment. Then have them list all the advantages that there might be.

8. Hold a class discussion and ask:

What was the most surprising item included in the furnishings?

Why is the closet important in a Japanese home?

Would you like to live in a house like this?

How is your home different from this apartment?

How would home size affect family relations? Give examples.

Which is more important, the furnishings or the space?

Follow-up:

1. Discuss with students the differences there might be if they were to furnish the apartment as if only teenagers lived in it. What difference would there be if two senior citizens lived in it?

2. Have students measure their own homes. How much space is there between the furniture? What does physical space in your home say about your need for space?

© CTIR
University of Denver

Title: **CULTURAL SELF-DEFENSE**

Introduction: Japanese culture has been subjected to many forces which might tear other cultures apart, such as foreign influence, rapid changes in technology, and limited space, but the Japanese have maintained a cohesive and vibrant culture in spite of these forces. This activity examines how the Japanese view foreigners in their country and points out Japan's ethnocentric behavior.

Objectives:

To define the concept of ethnocentrism
To define the concept of an alien
To draw conclusions about positive and negative effects of ethnocentrism

Grade Level: 7-12

Time: One class period

Materials: Handout #23, "US Woman Battles Japan Alien Policy"

Procedure:

1. Ask students the following questions:

    Have you ever met a person from a foreign country?

    Is there a part of your community where a large group of foreign people live? Have you ever gone to their church, eaten at their restaurants? How did it feel?

    What do you think about the Vietnamese "boat people" coming to your country? Should they be taken in? Are they a threat in any way?

2. Discuss the concept of an alien. List student responses on the chalk-board. How do we treat aliens?

3. Distribute Handout #23 and have students read the article.

4. After students have read the article, have a class discussion using the following questions as a guide:

    Why would the Japanese see aliens as a problem? Why are they worried? Which group of aliens are they especially concerned about? Why? Does this policy make sense due to the proximity of Koreans?

Why is it important for the Japanese to maintain their ethnic identity? Would this help their development?

List examples from the article of how the Japanese preserve their ethnicity.

What other factors would disturb Japanese culture besides aliens? How should the Japanese handle those problems?

Returning to the earlier discussion of Japanese stereotypes and aliens, what do you think about this policy? Is it right or wrong? Is it possible that the Japanese culture is much more complex than the stereotypes you listed? Do you feel that you are part of a culture? How important is it to you?

Follow-up:

1. Have students research to see if the same policy is in effect in Japan today. Present the reports in class.

2. Have students conduct research about the Japanese internment camps in the United States during World War II. Have students present the reports in class.

3. Research examples of ethnocentrism in your country's history. Did they ever welcome aliens? Why? What purpose did they serve for us?

4. Have students look into immigration policies and consider the following:

   Are we limiting foreign immigration? If so, why?

   Does official policy about immigration change with economic trends?

   Research the most recent immigration legislation.

Title: **CORPORATE CULTURES**

Introduction: Japan and Japanese business are becoming more and more important to the United States, as Japan is our largest trading partner after Canada. It is thus important to understand how Japanese business functions, especially since Japan's business structure is a key to Japanese society.

Objectives:

To define the concept "corporate culture"
To identify aspects of Japanese corporate culture
To analyze the positive and negative effects of corporate culture on the company and the individual worker
To hypothesize about the consequences of future corporate cultures

Grade Level: 10-12

Time: One class period

Materials: Handout #24, "A Hard Day's Night"
            Handout #25, "We Japanese"
            Handout #26, "IBM: The Colossus that Works"

Procedure:

1. Discuss the concept of school loyalty with the class. What does it mean to have school spirit? How do people show this spirit? What makes one school distinct from another? How do you serve your school? How does your school serve you?

2. Ask students if their parents or some other family member work for corporations. List the names of the corporations on the chalkboard. Discuss the difference between those that are multinational and those that are independent and/or small. Can you think of instances in which your family has shown corporate loyalty similar to school loyalty? What does the corporation do for your family? What makes one corporation different from other corporations (logos, product colors, ads, and so forth)?

3. Distribute Handout #24 and have students read the article. What are some of the instances in which the corporation is directly involved in the man's life? How much control does the corporation have over his life? Is the corporation the major force in his life? Is his family important to him? In what context?

4. Discuss with students how they would deal with the problem of family time vs. job time. How is the American conflict different from the Japanese conflict? Does it occur in all families and all corporations? If not, which corporations have these practices? Are they better corporations because of it?

5. Distribute Handout #25 to students and have them read the article. Discuss the article using the following questions. Is the man in the article loyal to his company? How? List examples of his loyalty on the chalkboard. Does this sort of relationship exist in the U.S.? What kinds of jobs might have this sort of relationship (principal-teacher, senior law partner to junior partner)? Are these relationships natural or artificial?

6. Write the word CULTURE on the chalkboard. Ask students to define the word. Try to reach a consensus on what it means.

7. Write the phrase "Corporate culture" on the chalkboard. From the two readings (and the definition of culture) try to define corporate culture. List the definitions on the chalkboard.

8. Distribute Handout #26 and have students read the material. Discuss using the following questions. What are some of the characteristics of IBM's corporate culture? What are the advantages and disadvantages of the corporate culture to the company? To the individual? How is IBM's corporate culture similar to corporate cultures in Japan? How is it different? Do the countries that each of these corporations are in have anything to do with the different corporate cultures?

9. Discuss with students whether they feel corporate cultures are good or bad. Why? Could a company's corporate culture conflict with another company's culture? How? How could corporate culture affect an individual who shifts jobs to another corporation? For instance, a move from Apple to IBM. What could happen in the future if all corporations created corporate cultures? What would happen to products? To employees? To advertising?

Follow-up:

1. Write to large corporations asking for logos, company songs, and other manifestations of corporate cultures. Try to write for American, European, and Japanese information. Compare the findings.

2. Ask a public relations executive from a local corporation to come to your classroom to give a presentation about that corporation's "image."

3. Have students bring in ads from large corporations. What do the ads try to say about the product and the company? Do you believe what the ads are trying to say?

4. Research different management techniques. What works best? Are corporate cultures efficient?

40

5. Explore multinational corporations in developing countries. Does management make any attempt to care for the workers? Are there corporate cultures in developing countries? Why or why not?

6. Research the corporate culture that emerged when Chrysler Corporation was "bailed out" by the United States government. What sacrifices did the workers make? How was the company's image changed? What other examples can you find?

Title: JAPAN'S ENERGY POLICY

Introduction: Japan's available energy resources are important to America and the world. According to an article in TIME MAGAZINE, Japan is America's second largest trading partner, after Canada, and is the world's second largest consumer of energy after the United States. Because Japan makes so many consumer goods, and because it takes energy to produce those goods, the world should be concerned about Japan's future energy policy.

Objectives:

To interpret a chart on Japanese energy sources
To construct graphs showing changing energy sources
To draw conclusions about Japan's energy problems
To synthesize data concerning Japan's proposed energy solutions

Grade Level: 7-12

Time: One class period

Materials: Handout #27, "Worksheet: Japan's Energy Policy"
            Graph paper
            Pencils

Procedure:

1. Have students bring a list from home of all the products in their houses that were made in Japan. Discuss the lists.

    What are some of the materials that go into making these products? Direct the discussion to the use of energy to produce the products.

    Did you realize that Japan is the second largest energy consumer in the world? Does this mean that the Japanese people consume a lot of energy? If not, what does it mean? Japan is the world's largest exporter of goods. Knowing that, what makes a nation a large energy consumer?

2. Distribute Handout #27 and have students complete Part I.

3. Have students complete Part II. What energy sources does Japan plan to use more of in the future? Less? According to the 1977 column, what source of energy accounted for most of Japan's energy consumption? Given these figures, what is the goal of Japan's energy policy? (To decrease the dependency on oil imports.)

43   © CTIR
                               University of Denver

4. Have students complete Part III. From where are the Japanese getting most of their oil? Is this a problem? Why?

5. Distribute graph paper to each student and have him/her make a bar graph illustrating Japan's energy policy. Using Part II of the handout, have students draw two bars for each type of energy, one for 1977 and one for 1995. The bar graphs should be labeled with the numbers from the worksheet. Students can graph the entire policy on one graph, or you can assign certain types of energy to different groups of students.

6. Using the graphs, hold a class discussion. Japan plans to significantly increase the use of which four energy sources? (Nuclear, new energy, imported coal, and liquid natural gas) Which energy source do they plan to increase the most?

   Why do you think the Japanese want to increase nuclear power production so much? Why is it a better resource than imported oil?

   From experience with nuclear energy in the United States and the USSR, is nuclear energy a good way to solve an energy dependence problem? Is energy dependency worse than the possible problems with nuclear energy? Why or why not?

   Given that there will be problems with nuclear power development, is it fair to let Japan bear the brunt of solving these problems so that other nations may buy luxury electrical items from Japan? Why or why not?

   How important are the solutions of Japan's energy problems to the development of Japan as a nation? (Remind students that the Japanese plan to nearly double their consumption of energy through 1995.) How important are the solutions to the further development of other nations?

   If nuclear power is cheaper to produce in terms of dollars and is less polluting than other forms of energy, what other "expense" might Japan have to pay in order to increase its production of nuclear energy? What trade-offs is Japan making?

Follow-up:

1. Hold similar discussions about resource dependency and trade-offs for new energy, imported coal, and liquid natural gas.

2. Have students find articles about what the Japanese think of the increased use of nuclear power.

3. Compare the developed world's consumption of energy with the developing world's consumption of energy. What conclusions can be drawn from this comparison?

4. Have students write an essay about cultural reactions to the use of energy. Do some cultures have negative feelings about artificially created power?

SOUTHEAST ASIA ACTIVITIES

Title: **SOUTHEAST ASIA PUZZLE**

Introduction: Southeast Asia is a vast, and geographically, culturally, and linguistically diverse region. In this activity, students will develop an understanding of the geographical makeup and diversity of this region.

Objectives:

To become familiar with the geography of Southeast Asia by reconstructing a
   puzzle map of the region
To learn the names of the nations of Southeast Asia
To learn the names of the oceans and seas of Southeast Asia
To classify the nations of the region as mainland or island nations

Grade Level: 5-8

Time: One to two class periods

Materials: Handout #28, "Map of Southeast Asia"; cut several copies into
            jigsaw puzzle pieces (thirty to forty each)
            World atlases

Procedure:

1. Divide class into small groups and distribute the puzzle pieces and
    atlases.

2. Have students put the puzzle maps together using the atlases.

3. Have students list:

    The names of countries and their capitals
    The oceans and seas of Southeast Asia
    Southeast Asian nations that are islands
    Southeast Asian nations that are on a continent
    Geographical features that make up the boundaries of the nations of
       Southeast Asia

Follow-up:

1. Explore the languages of Southeast Asia. Are there any geographical
    features that influence the prevalence or boundaries of these languages?

© CTIR
                                        University of Denver

Note: An excellent activity for teaching students about Southeast Asian languages and their linkages to other parts of the world may be found in Intercom #89, pages 11-23, published by The America Forum, 45 John Street, Suite 1200, New York, NY 10038.

2. Make a list of the resources--organic and mineral--in the Southeast Asian region. What do these nations export? What do they import?

3. Do similar puzzles and exercises for other regions of the world.

INDIA ACTIVITIES

Title: **IMPRESSIONS OF INDIA**

Introduction: We develop impressions of countries from a variety of sources. This activity allows students to see, share, and discuss their impressions of India. "Impressions of India" can be used as a springboard to the next activity entitled "Geography Puzzle."

Objectives:

To identify individual preconceptions of India
To discuss impressions of India
To analyze sources of impressions of India

Grade Level: 7-10

Time: One class period

Materials: 4 ft. by 6 ft. map of India, blank, and cut into five pieces
              Atlas or a large wall map of India
              Felt markers or colored pencils

Procedure:

1. Divide the class into five groups. Give each group a piece of the puzzle of India and ask each group to either write or draw their impressions of India on their piece of the puzzle.

2. After each group has completed this part of the assignment, have the groups put their pieces together to form the map of India. This puzzle may be placed on the floor, table, or bulletin board so that the entire class can see the map.

3. Have a representative from each group discuss their impressions with the rest of the class. Most of the students will probably mention topics like famine area, overpopulation, Ghandi, and so forth. As each group's impressions are discussed, write the topics on the chalkboard.

4. After the impressions have been written on the board, ask students:

    What were the sources of the impressions you have of India?

    How might an Indian do this activity with a map of our country?

    What similarities might there be between India and our country?

    What differences might there be between the two countries?

© CTIR
                                    University of Denver

Follow-up: Have students collect articles, pictures, or prepare reports from films, etc. on India that will either strengthen their impressions or clarify vague impressions, and that will give additional information to the class.

Title: **GEOGRAPHY PUZZLE**

Introduction: India is a subcontinent with diverse topography and climatic conditions. Geographic conditions have contributed to India's cultural diversity. Fourteen languages are recognized in the Constitution and 845 variations are spoken. This activity will acquaint students with India's geographic and cultured diversity.

Objectives:

To develop map skills
To recognize the impact of a diverse geography on the cultural development of India

Grade Level: 7-10

Time: One class period

Materials: Wall maps and atlases with a map of India
               Handout #29, "Indian Diversity Activity Sheet"

Procedure:

1. Divide the class into groups of three or four. Distribute Handout #29, and an atlas to each group. Have students locate the physical features and cities listed in Part I of the handout.

2. Have students complete Part II of the handout using the atlas.

3. Discuss the second part of the handout with students.

   How do the topographic features affect the population pattern and agricultural development of India?

   How might the geographic conditions of India influence its international relations with other countries?

   What are some of the problems posed for people in India by the diverse physical conditions?

   In what ways might the geographic setting have influenced the development of cultural differences?

© CTIR
                                                University of Denver

Follow-up:

1   Have students research different geographic regions and prepare a travel poster that could be placed on the classroom walls.

2.   Have students write one sentence describing what they have learned about the diversity of India. Compare the diversity to your country. How is diversity an advantage? Disadvantage? Have students analyze the saying, "Any truth can be found in India."

Title: UNDERDEVELOPED: MYTH OR REALITY?

Introduction: Students need to understand that "development" is defined by the developed world and that the "underdeveloped" nations may not agree with the perception. This activity will give students the opportunity to use the library, develop research skills, read and interpret charts, and develop conclusions concerning India's state as an underdeveloped or developed nation. These conclusions should be transferable to evaluation of the state of development of all countries.

Objectives:

To develop research skills
To read and interpret graphs and charts
To analyze data and draw conclusions about underdevelopment

Grade Level: 9-11

Time: Two class periods

Materials: Handout #30, "Student Activity Sheet"

Procedure:

1. Divide the class into groups of four or five. Ask each group to list at least five criteria they would use to determine if a country is developed or underdeveloped.

2. Briefly discuss each of the groups' criteria. Pose the problem of whether India is a developed or underdeveloped nation. What do most students think and why?

3. Divide the class into teams and distribute Handout #30. Instruct each group to find the answers to the questions in the library or resource center. (It is helpful if the teacher has all the possible research books pulled from the shelves and in a designated area of the library.) Remind the groups they are to work as teams. Allow at least one class period for research.

Follow-up: Debrief the questions from Handout #30 in a large group. List the different groups' conclusions on the board. Ask students the following:

Is it possible to apply the western definition of development to other countries?

© CTIR
University of Denver

Are there aspects of India that are developed? Underdeveloped?

How would you change your criteria to determine if a country is developed or underdeveloped?

Answers to Handout #30:

3. A. Religions: Buddhism, Hindu, Parsis, Zoroastrianism, Sikhs

    B. Influence of Indian philosophy in the United States today:
        1. Yoga 2. Meditation 3. Nonviolence (Martin Luther King)
        4. Doctrine of Karma 5. Reincarnation

    C. World famous architecture or art:
        1. Taj Majal 2. Red Fort 3. Ajanta 4. Sanchi 5. Bronze
        sculpture 6. Mughal art 7. Tile and stained glass

    D. Two world famous Indians (living or dead)
        1. Indira Gandhi 2. Mahatma Gandhi 3. Jawaharl Nehru 4. Buddha
        (Siddhartha Gautama)

Title: CIRCLE OF COMPLEXITIES

Introduction: Many suggestions can be made for solving India's complex problems. Students frequently make statements such as "India has a birth control problem" and offer simplistic suggestions as remedies. However, every solution has repercussions in other sectors of society. In this activity, students explore the repercussions and ramifications that relate to the solution of complex problems.

Objectives:

To recognize the complexity of problems facing India
To analyze the repercussions of proposed solutions to one problem on another area of the culture

Grade Level: 8-10

Time: One class period

Materials: Handout #31, "Circle of Complexity"
Handout #32, "Data Sheet"

Procedure:

1. Using the chalkboard, brainstorm about the problems in India. Some of the problems relate to industry, fuel, water, pollution, housing, disease, population, education, food, fertilizer, and health.

2. Distribute Handout #31 and have students write down the problems discussed on the lines on the chart. Distribute Handout #32 and have students expand the information on the "Circle of Complexity."

3. Hold a discussion regarding possible solutions to some problems. Suggest that one solution for one of the problems is providing tractors to all farmers. How does the solution affect the other areas? What happens to the small farmer? Where does the farmer get parts for the tractor? How does the farmer pay for the fuel costs (approximately $2.50 per liter)?

4. Another proposed solution may be the eradication of major diseases. How will this affect population? How will the food, fertilizer, education, and water be provided for the increased population?

5. Have a class discussion using the handouts as a basis for questions.

57

Title: **IMAGINARY LINES**

Introduction: The state is defined by political boundaries. The purpose of boundaries is to separate political states. Two types of boundaries exist: natural, and geometric (based on latitude and longitude). This activity will help students clarify India's boundaries and develop a sense of their stability.

Objectives:

To define types and classifications of boundaries
To illustrate boundary classifications with visual aids
To analyze the impact of boundaries on India's foreign policy

Grade Level: 8-10

Time: Two class periods

Materials: Two colored 5" squares and one colored circle for each student
               One black 1" x 8" strip of paper for each student
               Handout #33, "Seabed No Monopoly of Rich: Goehale"
               Handout #34, "Satellites for Global Observation"
               Handout #35, "Student Activity Sheet"
               Map of India

Procedure:

1. Present the following "classification" of boundaries* using the paper squares, circles, and strips for borders. Have students put a strip of paper on their desks and then put the two squares on either side. Explain that this type of border is called "Pioneer" and is prior to any settlement. Explain that the border between Canada and Alaska is an example of this type of border. "Why is this border considered the most stable? Can you think of any other examples?"

   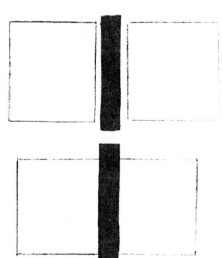

   Have students place the two paper squares on their desk and then put the border strip between them. Explain that this type of border is called "Antecedent" and exists before major settlement and societal development. An example of this border is Canada and the U.S. and India and Napal.

*This explanation of different types of borders is adapted from Political Geography by Norman Pounds, (NY: McGraw Book Co., Inc., 1963) p. 62.

"Why is this border stable? Can you name other examples?"

Have students put the two squares side by side, then place the circle so that it overlaps the two squares. Then have them put the black border strip on top, dividing the circle to illustrate the division. This type of border is called "Subsequent" and occurs after substantial development with attention given to cultural regions. An example of this border classification is that which exists between India and Pakistan. "What difficulties have developed between the countries since the Partition? Why is this border not as stable as the first two examples? Where are the cultural loyalties? Why can this border be a centripetal force?"

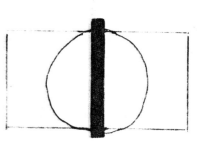

2. After students have discussed the different classifications of borders, discuss other types of boundaries using the following information. "Landscape" boundaries are deserts, mountains, rivers, etc. Are rivers always reliable boundaries? Why or why not? How might the Himalayas cause problems? Ocean boundaries present their own set of unique problems in that territorial claims to water vary from three to two hundred miles depending on the coastal nation in question. No standard limit is internationally recognized.

Distribute Handout #33 and have students read the article. After they have read the article, ask why ocean boundaries are of importance to India? Why would India be concerned with ocean pollution? Should everyone be concerned with this problem? Why or why not?

Discuss the increasing concern of the use or anticipated use of telecommunication equipment, space stations, satellites, nuclear weapons, etc. in space. Distribute Handout #34 and have students read the article. Who owns space? Why is space of concern to India?

3. Show students a large map of India that shows bordering nations. Are there any landlocked countries that border India? Why would India be concerned about its foreign policy with its landlocked neighbors? What "buffer" nations are between India and China? How would this affect India's foreign policy toward Butan and Nepal? Can you give examples of other nations that are between two strong nations?

4. Distribute Handout #35 and have students complete the handout using an atlas.

5. After students have completed the activity, hold a class discussion.

If you were President of India, what would your foreign policy alignment be based on India's borders?

© CTIR
University of Denver

Which countries would you want to have alliances and treaties with? Why?

India's official foreign policy is neutrality. Can India afford to remain neutral? What are some of the political, military, and economic pressures India must resist to remain neutral?

Why might India and the United States have a different view of China?

The United States gives military aid to Pakistan. How might this affect India-U.S. relations?

© CTIR
University of Denver

MIDEAST ACTIVITIES

Title: **THE PATRIOT**

Introduction: One of the phenomena about the Third World that is least understood by United States citizens is the negative reaction to Western influence found in a number of developing countries. The current Chinese campaign against "spiritual pollution" from the West, the crowds chanting anti-American slogans during the Iranian Revolution, and the abuse which some of our political leaders have faced in Latin America were all reactions to perceptions of cultural imperialism. This activity explores an alternative perspective on the Iranian Revolution, reasons for its anti-Western tone, and the influence of the media in shaping our perceptions. Excerpts from speeches and interviews of the Ayatollah Khomeini are analyzed in terms of our concepts of oppression and patriotism.

Objectives:

To identify reasons for negative reactions to Western influence in some developing countries
To analyze the relationship between religion and government in Islamic countries
To recognize the degree to which perceptions influence our view of Third World leaders.

Time: One or two class periods

Grade Level: 9-12

Materials: Handout #36, "The Patriot"

Procedure:

Part A

1. Discuss the general concept of oppression and the reasons oppressed people often revolt. Include a variety of forms of oppression, such as inequitable economic systems, censorship of books, magazines, and newspapers, repression of political opposition, use of terror squads and secret police, and military rule. List these on the board. Encourage students to give examples from a variety of revolutions such as those in France, the United States, China, the Soviet Union, and Central America.

2. Distribute Handout #36. Explain to the students that the reading consists of excerpts from speeches and interviews of a revolutionary leader in a Third World country. Their first task is to determine the leader's most serious criticisms of the current regime in his country.

65

3. In groups of three to five students, compile lists of criticisms of the current government. Ask each group to rank-order their list and then attempt to determine underlying causes for their top-ranked criticisms. For example, if a group lists the unequal distribution of oil wealth, an underlying cause may be ownership of the oil wells by foreigners.

4. Ask each group to report on its three top-ranking criticisms and their underlying causes. How many of these relate to foreign influence? What is the image of the current government that emerges? Would it survive without foreign support? What governments--contemporary or historical-- are the students reminded of? (Czarist Russia, El Salvador, Cuba, etc.) Is the concept of oppression only valid in relation to conservative governments or does it also apply to leftist governments? If you were a citizen of the country described, would this leader's speeches make you a revolutionary? How would your social, economic, and religious ties influence your decision? What defense of the criticisms might be offered by those supporting the current government? Who is most responsible for the oppression--the current government, or foreigners? Why?

Part B

1. Have students reread the handout, looking this time for evidence of the type of government that the leader would form if his or her side won the revolution.

2. In small groups, discuss the evidence and write a brief description of the type of government, including which groups would hold the most power, and what the major goals of the government would be (e.g., economic development, social justice, law and order).

3. After each small group has read its description to the class, summarize by using some or all of the following questions:

   Which word(s) best describe(s) the planned government?
      democracy
      communism
      socialism
      theocracy
      military junta
      monarchy

   In which sense is this plan of government revolutionary?

   In which sense is it reactionary?

   What current world governments does it resemble?

   What word or words in the reading might be used by the government to justify unlimited power?

   How does this form of government differ from that articulated in the U.S. Constitution?

© CTIR
University of Denver

1. Discuss the definition of the word <u>patriot</u>, including specific characteristics of historical or contemporary figures that students consider patriots.

2. Based on their impressions of the leader in their readings, ask students to decide whether or not they consider that person a patriot. List reasons for describing this leader as a patriot or not. Discuss how much individual and group perceptions determine our judgment on this issue. For example, to some American colonists, Thomas Paine was a patriot, while to others he was a "rabble-rouser." Robert E. Lee, Mao Zedong, and Gamal Abdul Nasser are other examples of leaders who were perceived differently from different perspectives.

3. Inform the students that the leader is actually the Ayatollah Khomeini of Iran. What parts of the reading agree with their preconceptions of Khomeini? Which do not? What factor(s) might account for the difference? Through which sources did the students receive most of their previous information about Khomeini?

Title: **THE VANISHING NOMAD**

Introduction: Change constantly affects different cultures, but one of the most marked changes has occurred with the nomads of the Middle East. In this activity, students will compare and contrast the lives of the nomads twenty or thirty years ago to the lives most of them are living today.

Objective:

To compare and contrast lives of nomads of the past and present
To become aware of constant changes in all cultures

Grade Level: 7-12

Time: Two class periods

Material: Handout #37, "Nomads Settling Down"

Procedure:

1. Discuss with students the concept of "change." Include discussions of housing, economics, lifestyles, education, and medical care. Is change negative or positive? Why?

2. Distribute Handout #37 and have students read. Discuss the article with students.

3. Divide students into groups of four or five. Assign each group a different country that has or has had nomads (such as Jordan and Saudi Arabia), and have them do library research into past lifestyles and compare and contrast that with current lifestyles. Students are to prepare reports for class presentation.

4. Have each group present their reports to the class.

5. After the presentations, hold a class discussion. In what areas have there been the greatest changes? What are the negative aspects of the changes? Positive aspects? Compare the changes between the various countries.

Follow-up: Have students compare and contrast nomad lifestyles with those of aboriginal populations from North America (Native Americans). Present the report in class.

                              © CTIR
University of Denver

AFRICA ACTIVITIES

Title: **THE DOCTORS OF NIGERIA**

Introduction: When studying a culture, it is not enough to examine its static qualities. The dynamics of the culture--how it reacts to outside forces--are just as important. The film "The Doctors of Nigeria," produced by WGBH in Boston (NOVA), portrays the impact development has had on the Nigerian culture, and it explores the ways in which Nigerians have struggled to maintain their culture in the face of twentieth century medical advances. This is a positive film, one which shows that development is not always a bad thing, and that community, national, and worldwide efforts can produce solutions to cultural problems.

Objectives:

To understand and appreciate the Nigerian medical system
To develop analytical film-watching skills
To define the Nigerian development cycle as it pertains to medicine

Grade Level: 7-12

Time: One class period

Materials: Film "The Doctors of Nigeria." Check at a nearby film library such as at a university or public library. This film may also be rented from Time-Life Video, 100 Eisenhower Drive, Paramus, NJ 07652, 201/843-4545, at a price of approximately $90.00 for three days.
Large wall map of Africa

Procedure:

1. Ask students the following questions: What are some technological changes which affected your grandparents' lives? How does modernization change people's lives? Do your grandparents or parents ever long for the "good ole days?" Have there been any radical changes in technology in your lifetime? Have you ever thought about what modernization might do to someone's life or culture if that person has never been exposed to modern technology before?

2. Explain to students that they will be watching a documentary film about modernization in a developing country, and that they will see some of the problems technology causes in various parts of the world.

Show the map of Africa and point out Nigeria. Explain that Nigeria is a developing country with many old traditions. It is facing some radical changes which are affecting the old traditions. Its people are trying to

© CTIR
                                                    University of Denver

accommodate those changes. The movie talks about traditional healing (witch doctors) and modern healing (modern medical science). Have students brainstorm words they think characterize witch doctors. List these on the chalkboard. Have students brainstorm words they feel characterize modern medicine and list these on the chalkboard.

3. Preview some of the specific terms from the movie, using the map of Africa if necessary. The terms are: Lagos, the capital city located in the southwest; WHO, the World Health Organization, an agency associated with the UN; British colonialism which lasted from 1861-1960, (this is why many Nigerians speak English and the reason it is the official language); Yoruba, name of a language and ethnic group located in western Nigeria; Ibo, a language and ethnic group located in eastern Nigeria; Hausa-Falani, collection of tribes in northern Nigeria whose language is Hausa; Civil War which lasted from 1967 to 1970--the southern section tried to secede and became the Republic of Biafra--the attempt was not successful.

4. Show the movie. After viewing the movie, hold a class discussion using the following questions as a guide.

How are Nigerians different from Americans? Similar?

Have you ever seen a movie about Nigeria before? What did you think of it? Did anything surprise you?

How did the Nigerians merge old ways with new ways? (Marketing of traditional herbal drugs; university scientists collaborating with traditional healers; Nigerian patients visiting both orthodox and traditional doctors; inviting traditional healers to the groundbreaking ceremony; mothers chanting songs at Well-Baby Day; and building a well in a village community.)

What are your reactions to traditional healers? Are they mere witch doctors, or something more? Compare your new reactions with your lists on the board. What words would you strike from the list? What words would you add? Do you now have more respect for the traditional healers? Did it look like they knew what they were doing? Do their practices make sense? Could modern medicine learn from traditional healers?

If the Nigerians had stopped the traditional healers from practicing, what might have happened in Nigeria? How would the Nigerians have reacted? How important are traditional healers to patients' states of mind? How important is it for you to trust the doctor you go to?

5. List on the chalkboard the cycle Nigeria went through in its medical practices. Have students try to determine the cycle from the knowledge they gained from the movie.

Traditional
Healing

Modern
Medicine

Non-Traditional
Healing--British
Colonialism

6. Do you think Nigeria has a modern medical system? Compare your new
reactions with your lists on the chalkboard. What words would you strike
from the list? What words would you add? What do you mean by modern? Is
modern medicine in Nigeria necessarily like modern medicine in the United
States?

Title: **DIALECTICAL DIVERSITY**

Introduction: Africa is a fascinating continent. Linguistically, it is one of the most complex areas in the world. The usual figure of 800 languages for the continent is doubtless an underestimate. African linguistics is the springboard for many other areas of study, such as anthropology, geography, even politics. This activity provides students with a simplified linguistic map of Africa and introduces them to the relationship between language and culture. Other relationships could be studied as well, limited only by students' imaginations.

Objectives:

To examine the effects of linguistic diversity on African history and culture
To analyze the relationship between language and culture in Africa
To compare language families in Africa with cultural areas in Africa
To brainstorm ways of using linguistics in the study of Africa

Grade Level: 9-12

Time: One class period

Materials: Large classroom map of Africa
             Handout #38, "Language Families of Africa" (make transparency) for
                 your use
             Handout #39, "Cultural Areas of Africa" (make transparency) for
                 your use
             Overhead projector

Procedure:

1. Discuss languages with students using the following questions as a guide:

   How many languages do you speak?

   How many languages are spoken in the United States?

   Is English really the native language of North America? Why is English
   the main language in the U.S. if it is not the native language?

   What does the fact that English is the dominant language in the United
   States say about U.S. history?

2. Display the classroom map of Africa. Ask students if they know how many
   languages are spoken in Africa. Tell students that over 800 recognized
   languages are spoken there, along with countless dialects. What do you
   think this fact implies about African history and African cultures?

3. Illuminate the transparency of Handout #38 on an overhead projector. Explain to students that families 1-7 are major language groups. Have a student locate them on the map. Do the names of the families tell you anything? (For example, the Afro-asiatic family is located in the north near the Asian continent.)

    Families 8-12 are minor families. How do you suppose these languages arose? Why didn't they combine with other families? Why would a group of people want to maintain their own language?

    What is the main language family in Africa? (Niger Congo) What cultural areas does it encompass? Why would people living in these regions be more likely to speak similar languages than people living in the northern sections of Africa? (The desert is a barrier to language transferral, the Asians have a heavier influence in the north, etc.)

4. Have students discuss and list on the chalkboard problems that this language diversity might cause.

5. Illuminate Handout #39. Have students compare it with the geographical features on the large map of Africa. What does this imply about culture? (That it is connected with geography.) Discuss with students how someone in the desert would live differently from someone who lives in the Congo. List those items which make up a culture in addition to geography and languages.

6. Have students compare the two maps. Are there any language families which correspond roughly with the culture groups? Which language families encompass more than one culture area? List the comparable language and cultural groups on the chalkboard.

7. Discuss with students why cultural conflict is a special problem in Africa. What problems might arise in a single nation if its people speak dozens of languages? List these problems on the chalkboard. Americans have a Spanish-English language conflict, but is it as significant as the African conflict? What are some solutions to this conflict? Has colonization by European nations had an affect on language problems in Africa? How? The study of English-language dominance in the United States says something about U.S. history. What could the study of African language families teach us about Africa? What areas of study other than history could we learn about?

Follow-up:

1. Divide students into four groups and have each group choose one of the following activities to complete and present to the class:

    a. Make a language family map for Western Europe. Have students compare the language map to the geographical features of Europe.

© CTIR
University of Denver

b. Make a language tree of Indo-European languages. Most dictionaries have language charts that might be helpful.

c. Prepare a report about any African nation and its language policies. Have students consider what the official language is and whether the nation encourages diversity. Also consider languages taught in the schools, colonial impact on language, and what language the elite group(s) speak(s).

d. Compare the natural cultural-linguistic groups in Africa with the artificial nations created by colonialism. Discuss the type of impact colonialism had on African culture, and the effect of natural borders on tribal or linguistic groups.

© CTIR
University of Denver

Title: _____ , THIS IS YOUR LIFE

Introduction: Every nation has a unique cultural heritage. Students in the United States are deluged with information concerning the U.S heritage, and they are taught to be proud of their unique position in history. This activity will help students realize that the histories of other nations are just as unique.

Objectives:

To compare the historical development of Nigeria and the United States
To increase awareness of western ignorance of the histories of developing nations
To evaluate the benefits and limitations of comparative history

Grade Level: 9-12

Time: One class period

Materials: Handout #40, "_____ , This Is Your Life"
           Handout #41, "Nigeria and United States: This Is Your Life"

Procedure:

1. Distribute Handout #40 and ask students to read it carefully. Then ask them to write on a piece of paper what nation they think the handout is discussing. Tabulate the results on the chalkboard.

2. If the United States is the unanimous "winner," ask students if any other possibilities exist.

3. Distribute Handout #41 and inform students that the country they just read about is the African nation of Nigeria. Have students read the handout.

4. Discuss the handout and students' reactions.

   How is Nigeria like the United States? List student answers on the chalkboard. How is Nigeria different? Again, list the answers on the board.

   Why did you first think of the United States when you read the first handout? How important is the study of United States history? Is the study of other countries' histories important to us? Why or why not?

   How does a study comparing other countries' histories with our own help us understand the issues of development? What are the disadvantages?

Title: **COLOR ME POLITICAL**

Introduction: Not only do developing countries face economic problems, but political problems as well. Nigeria is no exception. Nigeria's political history has undergone tremendous changes: from tribal governments, to colonial rule, to independence, to military dictatorship, to civil war, to constitutional government, and back to military rule. This activity focuses on the period before the recent coup when Nigeria was trying to overcome some of its ethnic problems.

Because Nigeria has a long history of ethnic rivalry, political development is hampered by the lack of national unity. The three main ethnic groups in Nigeria are located in three separate geographic regions. Moreover, the three groups vote in distinct ethnic blocs. This activity proves that. Students will see that ethnic tension is one political problem for African nations.

Objectives:

To analyze the geographic and ethnic bases for the three main political parties in Nigeria
To reinforce chart and map skills
To draw conclusions about the problems facing an ethnically diverse developing nation

Grade Level: 10-12

Time: One class period

Materials: Handout #42, "Nigeria's Election Returns Shagari to Power"
Handout #43, "Nigeria's Nineteen States""
Handout #44, "Nigerian Presidential Election Results"
Colored pencils for each student (5 colors for each)

Procedure:

1. Distribute Handout #42 and read out loud. Help students become familiar with the names and geographic regions of the ethnic groups. Distribute Handout #43 to help students become familiar with the groups. The Hausa-Falani Tribe lives in northern Nigeria, and they are led by Shagari of the NPN party. The Yoruba live in western Nigeria, and their political leader is Awolowo of the UPN party. The Ibo live in southeastern Nigeria and are led by Azikiwe of the NPP party.

2. Distribute Handout #44 and have students circle in pen all percentages above thirty. Ask students to count how many states show significant percentages (over 30), for more than one party (only 6). How many show

© CTIR
University of Denver

overwhelming percentages (over 60), for one party (13)? What does this say about party leanings in Nigerian states?

3. Assign a different color pencil for each of the political parties and have students transfer the circled data from Handout #44 to the map on Handout #43. If possible, use two different tints of the same color for the NPN and the PRP, since the PRP is a splinter party of the NPN. Students should shade in the color of the winning party for each state. For the six states which split the vote between two parties, shade in the color of the party getting the most votes, and make hatch marks for the party getting the second highest number of votes.

4. Discuss the results indicated on the student maps.

What do your maps look like? What are the outstanding characteristics? Are the colors scattered all over, or are they concentrated in a particular area? Refer to the article. Which tribes are located where in Nigeria? Where are the parties located?

Which party is dominant in Nigeria? Which tribe or ethnic group is, therefore, dominant? What political problem do you see on your map?

Different states vote in blocs in the United States, but they don't necessarily have a political problem. Why is Nigeria different?

Nigeria has many complex governmental and party rules to insure national unity. Why is this unnecessary in the U.S.? Why would other developing countries have to have complex constitutions like this one?

Follow-up: Have students look in newspapers for information about elections in other developing countries. Try to determine from the articles what types of political problems these countries might have.

Title: A MAN FOR ALL SEASONS

Introduction: Developing nations not only have developing economies, but also developing political systems. Various factors in developing countries cause political leaders to act differently than political leaders in the industrialized democracies. The President of Nigeria, Shehu Shagari, for instance, must lead an ethnically torn country, oversee the exportation of crude oil, improve the standard of living for his people, and steer a careful foreign policy as the leader of an important African nation. This activity illustrates the importance of political support for less developed nations.

Objectives:

To evaluate a reading for bias
To make inferences about the frame of reference of a reading
To analyze the relationship between government and big business in a
  developing country

Grade Level: 9-12

Time: One class period

Materials: Handout #45, "A President for all Seasons"

Procedure:

1. Discuss with students the meaning of bias. Write the definition on the board. Do nations have biases? Can you give examples? How do these biases affect political systems?

2. Distribute Handout #45 and have students read. Ask students to underline all the biased statements in the article.

3. After students are through reading the article, discuss the statements that were biased. Write their answers on the board.

4. Discuss the article with students. Did you notice this article is actually an advertisement? Point out paragraph No. 5 and ask if it accurately reports the President's policies and actions. Who do you think wrote this article? According to the article, what is the most important problem facing Shagari? The magazine from which the article was taken is distributed over the entire continent. Why would an advertiser want to show the President as a good guy? What is the advertiser selling in this ad? Is it possible that the ad is merely what it seems to be--praise for a president? Why would a president need this sort of positive publicity? Does he need it in Nigeria? In Africa? In the world?

5. Divide students into groups of four or five and have each group write an advertisement for the president or leader of your country. After they are through, have each group present their ad to the others. What are the biases used? How did each of them want the country to see the president? What do political campaign ads point out about the candidates?

© CTIR
University of Denver

LATIN AMERICA ACTIVITIES

<u>Title</u>: **MISSING**

<u>Introduction</u>: Many students in the United States and Canada have no conception of political repression. They do not understand the fear or inactivity of those whose rights have been suppressed. This "why don't they <u>do</u> something" attitude needs to be tempered with an understanding of just <u>what</u> goes on in these peoples' lives. This human rights simulation will help students feel the fear and indecision facing people who live in politically repressive states. Hopefully, it will also give them an appreciation of the freedoms in their own country. (Note: this simulation has a definite Latin American tint to it, but this does not mean that Latin America has a monopoly on human rights violations, nor that all Latin American governments are repressive.)

<u>Objectives</u>:

To define the concept of "political rights"
To simulate the psychological and physical pressure of political repression
To draw conclusions about the impact of domestic and global counter pressure
   on a repressive government

<u>Grade Level</u>: 7-12

<u>Time</u>: One class period

<u>Materials</u>:   Handout #46, "Juan Verdad: Editor"
                Handout #47, "Rules and Guidelines"
                Handout #48, "Roles"
                Handout #49, "Missing Narrative"
                Handout #50, "Supremia Herald"

<u>Procedure</u>:

1. Discuss the meaning of the word "rights." What is a right? Who has rights? What are human rights? On the chalkboard write: political, economic, and social. What are the rights that fit into these three categories? Do the African countries place more importance on economic rights than political rights? Why? Which rights are most important for Central and South America? Why?

   Look at the list of political rights. Ask: do all countries have political rights? Which countries do? Do not?

2. Explain to students that they are going to take part in a simulation about political rights. Distribute Handout #46 and read it out loud. Then distribute Handout #47 and read it aloud. Make sure that students understand what is expected of them.

3. Assign roles to each student, Handout #48. Double up on some roles if necessary, e.g., social workers, nuns, priests, sons, daughters. Name tags might help students to keep track of everyone. Give students time to study their roles.

4. Read the narrative of Handout #49 out loud to students. Whenever it reaches "What should you do next?," carefully review the options available to the students, but do not tell them the consequences until after they have decided. Remind students to stay in their "roles" when making their decisions. Some students may prefer to think up their own options. In that case, the teacher will have to decide what the consequences should be.

    During the second set of options, some students might choose Option A and will end up missing. Tell them to stand in a separate part of the classroom until they return to the game later in the narrative. During the very last set of options, many of the students will end up in jail. Keep those in jail separate from those who are missing, and also separate them from those who are still free.

5. When the narrative calls for it, distribute Handout #50 to everyone, regardless of their status. It contains information that will be useful to students in the discussion following the end of the game.

6. At the end of the simulation, <u>arbitrarily</u> release one-half of the jailed participants. During the evaluation questions, leave the jailed searchers separate from the freed searchers so that the students can visualize the simulation's ending.

7. Hold a class discussion or evaluation using the following questions.

    Why do you suppose the simulation ends here? Who is still in jail? What has changed since the simulation began? Does the ending make any sense?

    What has happened to the Indigis (the ones whose rights were originally suppressed)? Are they any better off? Will they ever be any better off? In the simulation, which story did the media cover, Verdad's disappearance or the Indigi massacres? Why? Can you think of any real-life cases in which native people are suppressed (e.g., U.S., Australia, Brazil, South Africa, Romania)?

    List the rights which were denied in the simulation. What type of rights are they? Why do you think the authorities had to take the action they did? Are governments ever justified in denying political rights? In which cases? Would people with money have any of their rights denied? If they were put in jail would they have a greater chance of getting out because of money and/or influence?

    Were there any risks which had "good" consequences? (You may have to examine both the option-consequences sections, as well as the narrative itself.) Which risks had consequences that were "okay"? Which did not?

90

CTIR
University of Denver

Was it hard to figure out which options to choose? Did the decisions become easier to make once you had figured out what the government response would be? If you had lived in such a country all your life, how would this affect your political life? Would you _ever_ take risks?

Which factors were the most important leading to Verdad's eventual release? Least important? Was Supremian pressure more important than domestic pressure? What does this say about the foreign policy of powerful countries? Do individuals in powerful countries have a responsibility to individuals in smaller, repressive countries? Why or why not?

Was this simulation realistic? How might money have an affect on the outcome? Does this simulation remind you of any real life situations? Would you like to live in Barbarica? Why or why not? Have your feelings about life in your own country changed? How?

Follow-up:

1. Have students read books about human rights violations (check the bibliography for some references). Have a class discussion about the books, or have students write a report analyzing which rights were denied, what actions were taken, and who was or should have been responsible for alleviating the problems.

2. Have students collect news articles about human rights violations and the government's response to them. What factors prevent them from acting?

© CTIR
University of Denver

Title: **CENTRAL AMERICAN POWER PLAY**

Introduction: One of the key issues in developing countries is the distribution of wealth and influence. It is often seen as a power play between the elite and the rest of society. In this activity groups of students role play a confrontation between the powerful and the powerless in a Central American society and predict what will happen to that society by the year 1995. An optional extension is a simulation of a peace conference in which students assume the roles of regional and international actors and attempt to reach a compromise. Students should have some background on Central America and access to current information on the region.

Objectives:

To gather information on the social structure of a Central American country, including sources of power, land ownership, and historical relationships
To role play a confrontation between the powerful and the powerless in one Central American country
To analyze the relationship between the powerful and the powerless in that country, in Central America, and in the Third World in general
To negotiate a compromise between groups representing the major actors in the Central American crisis

Grade Level: 9-12

Time: Three to five class periods

Materials: Handout #51, "Power Play: A Central American Drama"
Resources for research on Central America (current periodicals, reference works, economic and social analyses); also see bibliography

Procedure:

1. Ask students to write five words or phrases that they think of when they hear the word power. Discuss their answers, pointing out how they reflect different sources and uses of power.

2. Have a class discussion about power in your society using the following questions:

Adapted from an activity by Dr. John McCammant of the Graduate School of International Studies, University of Denver. Used with permission.

How do people gain power in our society?

Is it more common to inherit power or to achieve it through individual effort?

Who are the powerless in your society?

What is the nature of the relationship between the powerful and the powerless in your country?

Give examples of confrontations between the powerful and the powerless in your history, current affairs, and in your own community.

3. Introduce the subject of the role play on Central America by distributing Handout #51. Discuss why it is called "Power Play." Ask students to predict patterns of distribution of land and wealth and alliances between specific groups within the country.

4. As a class, decide on the country in which the play will be set, which groups will be represented, and which will be designated the powerful and the powerless. (Some groups, such as women and children, may be split.) Set up groups and assign roles. Allow time for research and for planning meetings within each larger group--the powerful and the powerless. Assist students in writing the scripts for Scenes I and II.

5. Select representatives of each group to meet with the teacher to identify the specific confrontation situation that will be the focus of Scene III. The nature of the confrontation will depend on the country chosen, current issues in that country, and the level of sophistication of the students. Some suggestions which may be suitable are listed below:

Intervention of a foreign power (U.S., Cuba, Soviet Union, or a neighboring country).

Visit of the Pope.

Election of a president or legislature.

Land reform proposal.

Assist students in writing a script which sets up the confrontation. Leave the actual confrontation open-ended to allow for improvisation.

6. Perform Scenes I, II, and III. During Scene III, allow students to role play the confrontation, but stop it before a resolution.

7. Have each student write his or her own version of Scene IV, the Conclusion. Each conclusion would include how the confrontation will end and what will happen to the power structure of the country by the year 1995. Encourage students to use specific information and understanding of the perspectives of each group to make valid predictions.

8. After the scenes have been played, discuss students' conclusions, emphasizing the nature of the relationship between the powerful and the powerless. Select from the following questions to debrief the play.

Which forms of power were the strongest?

What were the most serious problems of the powerless?

How is power distributed? How is it used?

What are the most effective strategies for the powerless to use?

What options are open to both groups in the next ten years?

What is the role of the United States government and multinational corporations in the balance of economic power in Central America? What options are open to U.S. government officials and leaders of multinational corporations in the next ten years?

Could the play you wrote be adapted to take place in the United States? Why or why not?

Could it take place in other Central American countries? In other Third World countries that you have studied? What are some of the differences and similarities among the power structures of Central American countries? Among the Third World countries?

Compare the situation in the play to one or more of these historical situations:

> Czarist Russia
> Vietnam after World War II
> Cuba under Batista
> Ireland in the twentieth century
> Medieval Europe
> Brazil today
> China during the Cultural Revolution
> Invasion of Panama by the United States

Optional Extension:

1. Discuss the importance of compromise and negotiation in conflict situations. Assign students to each of the following roles:

> Government of El Salvador
> U.S. Government
> Contadora Nations
> Nicaraguan Government
> Cuba and the Soviet Union

© CTIR
University of Denver

2. Review the most recent developments in Central America and previous attempts to resolve the conflict (Contadora proposals, etc.). Ask each group to prepare and present to a simulated "peace conference" a brief position paper outlining its interests in the conflict and points that should be included in a peace agreement. (The conference may be named after the town or school, and props such as flags and slogans may be used. Several students may be assigned to be reporters responsible for publishing short news articles on the conference from the point of view of their countries.)

3. Regroup so that one representative of each role is included in each small group (i.e., each small group will have one El Salvadorian government official, one U.S. diplomat, one Contadora representative, one Nicaraguan government official, and one Cuban or Soviet diplomat). Ask each group to work out a compromise among its members, each of whom will try to influence the others to accept provisions favorable to his side in the conflict. Have the small groups present their compromises to the class. Vote on which compromise the students consider most likely to lead to a peaceful resolution of the conflict in Central America. Hold a simulated signing of the peace agreement.

Follow-up:

1. Invite a refugee from Central America to speak to the class.

2. Write to the U.S. State Department for its position paper on Central America.

3. Invite a representative from a multinational corporation with interests in Central America to speak to the class.

4. Have students research the relationship between military policy and economic policy in Central America.

5. Write letters expressing a position on the issues to political representatives.

BIBLIOGRAPHY

RESOURCES AND REFERENCES

Following are just a few suggested resources and references. It is suggested that the teacher make use of the school library and other local resources.

Achebe, Chinua. Things Fall Apart. Greenwich, CT: Faucett Publishers, 1959.

Amnesty, International. Annual Reports.

>   These readable country-by-country summaries by a human rights activist organization are good student sources of information on violations of human rights in Central America. Published annually and available in most libraries.

Archibald, R.M. and Pollock, David H. (eds.). Latin American Prospects for the 1980s. NY: Praeger, 1983.

Brandt, Willy. North-South: A Programme for Survival. Cambridge, MA: MIT Press, 1982.

Davis, Shelton H. and Hodson, Julie. Witnesses to Political Violence in Guatemala. Boston: Oxfam America, 1982.

>   Personal accounts of persons who have worked in rural development in Guatemala. Includes evidence of repression of peasant groups.

Dingal, John and Landau. Assassination on Embassy Row. NY: Pantheon, 1980.

Dore, Ronald and Mars, Zoe (eds.). Community Development: Comparative Case Studies in India, The Republic of Korea, Mexico and Tanzania. London: Croom Helm, 1981.

Eguchi, Yujiro. "Japanese Energy Policy," International Affairs (Spring 1980).

Franda, Marcus F. India's Rural Development: An Assessment of Attempts. Bloomington, IN: American University Field Staff, Indiana University Press, 1979.

Galtung, Johan. Development, Environment and Technology: Toward a Technology for Self-Reliance. NY: United Nations, 1979.

Glassner, Martin I. (ed.). Global Resources: Challenges of Interdependence. NY: Praeger, 1983.

Halloran, Richard. Japan: Images and Realities. Tokyo: Tuttle, 1970.

Hardgrave, Robert C. India: Government and Politics in a Developing Nation. 2nd edition. NY: Harcourt Brace Jovanovich, 1975.

Hawley, W.M. Chinese Folk Designs: A Collection of 300 Cut-Paper Designs. NY: Dover, 1971.

Hyden, Goran. No Shortcuts to Progress: African Development Management in
Perspective. Berkeley: University of California Press, 1983.

Japan Economic Institute of America. Japan's Industrial Policies: What Are
They, Do They Matter and Are They Different from Those in the United States?
Washington, D.C.: Author, 1984.

Khomeini, Imam. Translated and Annotated by Hamid Algar. Islam and Revolution.
Berkeley: Mizan Press, 1981.

Kogare, Yoshihiro (ed.). Changing Value Patterns and Their Impact on Economic
Structure: A Report to the OECD. Tokyo: University of Tokyo Press, 1982.

Kublin, Hyman. India. Boston: Houghton-Mifflin, 1972.

Kuo, Nancy. Chinese Paper-Cut Designs: Old and Modern. London: Alec
Tiranti, 1964.

Levine, Solomon B. Human Resources in Japanese Industrial Development.
Princeton, NJ: Princeton University Press, 1980.

Lernoux, Penny. Cry of the People. Garden City, NY: Doubleday, 1980.

    Focuses on the Catholic Church in Central America. Readable, includes
    details on persecution of priests, nuns, and lay workers. Now available in
    paperback by Penguin.

Morris, Arthur S. Latin American Economic Development and Regulated
Differentiation. Totowa, NJ: Barnes & Noble, 1981.

NBC News. Central America in Turmoil. NY: Author, 1983.

    This pamphlet contains basic information on each Central American country,
    insurgency movements, and U.S. involvement. It may be ordered from NBC
    News, 30 Rockefeller Plaza, NY, NY 10020.

Panikar, P.G.K. Population Growth and Agricultural Development. Rome: Food
and Agricultural Organization of the UN, 1978.

Pounds, Norman. Political Geography. NY: McGraw Book Co., Inc., 1963.

Preston, Julia. "Guatemala, The Muffled Scream." Mother Jones (November
1981).

Rosengren, Frank H., Wiley, Marylee C. and Wiley, David S., Internationalizing
Your School: A Handbook and Resource Guide. NY: National Council on Foreign
Language and International Studies, 1983.

Schlesinger, Stephen and Kinzer, Stephen. Bitter Fruit, the Untold Story of the American Coup in Guatemala. Garden City, NY: Doubleday, 1982.

Historical account of the role of the CIA and multinational corporations in Guatemala in 1954. Includes a summary of recent events.

Schultz, George. "Strengthening Democracy in Central America." Washington, DC: Department of State, 1983. (Current Policy No. 468, Bureau of Public Affairs.)

Official U.S. policy in Central America, including rationale and assessment of the economic and political situation.

Sidel, Ruth. Families of Fengsheng; Urban Life in China. Baltimore: Penguin, 1974.

Although somewhat dated, useful for a personalized view of the role of the neighborhood committee in China's cities.

Timerman, Jacobo. Translated by Toby Talbot. Prisoner Without A Name, Cell Without A Number. NY: Vintage, 1982.

Townsend, James R. and Bush, Richard C. The People's Republic of China: A Basic Handbook. NY: Council on International and Public Affairs and the China Council of the Asia Society, 1982.

Contains up-to-date data on administrative structure of local government in the People's Republic of China.

U.S. House of Representatives. "Human Rights in Guatemala." Washington, D.C.: Government Printing Office, July 30, 1984.

Hearings before the subcommitees on Human Rights and International Organizations and on Inter-American Affairs of the Committee on Foreign Affairs of the House of Representatives, Ninety-Seventh Congress, First Session. July 30.

Vogel, Ezra F. Japan's New Middle Class: The Salary Man and His Family in a Tokyo Suburb. Berkeley: University of California Press, 1971.

Wai, Dunstan M. (ed.). Interdependence in A World of Unequals. Boulder, CO: Westview, 1982.

Weiner, Myron. India at the Polls: The Parliamentary Elections of 1977. Washington, D.C.: American Enterprise Institute for Public Policy Research, 1978.

Wyria, Gary W. The Politics of Latin American Development. NY: Cambridge University Press, 1984.

PERIODICALS

Development. Published by the Society for International Development.

Central American Update. A bimonthly publication which provides current coverage on events in Central America. It may be ordered from Central American Update, Box 2207, Station P, Toronto, Ontario, Canada M5 2T2. ($10.00 per year)

GEO. Published by GEO Publishing Company, Los Angeles, CA 90036. Published monthly. ($29.95 per year)

Global Perspectives. Published by Global Perspectives in Education, Inc., New York, NY 10003. Also publishes Intercoms on various global issues.

Latin American Update. A bimonthly publication of the Washington Office on Latin America, 110 Maryland Avenue, NE, Washington, DC 20002. ($10.00 per year) February 1983 issue focused on Guatemala.

National Geographic. Published by the National Geographic Society, Washington, D.C. 20036. ($15 per year)

Newsweek has also produced materials on Central America for use in schools. Check with their educational division for their latest materials.

STUDENT HANDOUTS

AIR-INDIA

Everything about Air-India's daily flights to New York is big. Big-hearted welcome, big jumbo space, big choice of gourmet foods and a big cabin crew of gentle hostesses and helpful pursers.
Distant places seem nearer when you fly Air-India. Maybe it's the luxurious and distinctive fleet of 747s. Maybe it's the convenient flight schedules to 44 cities around the world. Maybe it's the gentle hostess who serves you as if you were the only guest.
It's all this and more that makes Air-India's Orient Express the orient express.

AIR-INDIA
Window to a different world.

_____
Used with permission of Air-Orient.

NORTHWEST ORIENT

Fly the Orient Express Way

**Nobody flies to the Orient direct
from more U.S. cities**

Only Northwest flies from 11 major U.S. cities to the Orient
with no plane change en route. And only Northwest — nobody
else — can give you convenient connections from 28 other
Northwest cities.

Nobody else flies more 747s to the Orient (21 each week) and
gives you the choice of Polar, North-Pacific, and Mid-Pacific
routes. Or gives you magnificent Regal Imperial service —
including movies* and stereo* — while you're in flight.

Fly the Orient Express Way to Tokyo, Osaka, Seoul, Okinawa,
Taipei, Manila, Hong Kong. Nobody else does it nearly so well.

*$2.50 charge on international 747 flights

 **NORTHWEST ORIENT 747**

Used with permission of Northwest Orient Airlines.

10,000 NIGERIAN STUDENTS ARE STRANDED IN U.S.

New York (A))--At least 10,000 Nigerian students are stranded on American campuses without money for tuition or living expenses because of delays in scholarship funding from their homeland, university officials say.

American officials blame the delay on the Nigerian government's response to an economic pinch, while a Nigerian official attributes it to bureaucratic errors. But whatever the cause, the students without funds have been barred from registering for classes at hundreds of colleges and universities this fall.

That leaves the students, who cannot work under U.S. immigration rules, in violation of their student visas and subject to deportation, officials said.

Julie Rose of Iowa State University, coordinator for Nigerian students for the National Association for Foreign Students, said 10,000 to 13,000 Nigerian students--about half the Nigerian students in the country--have not received their scholarship funds.

She said those students will be unable to pay their tuition, rent and utilities or buy books or even food as the fall semester begins later this month. The students owe $22 million in tuition and $65 million in living expenses to hundred of colleges and universities, she said.

Rose said each school where Nigerian students are in default is handling the problem on its own. She said most universities are not allowing the students to register for classes this fall if they still owe for last year, though some require all students to pay at least part of this semester's fees in advance.

At the University of Wisconsin-Stout, where 50 of the 135 Nigerian students need $750,000 to pay their tuition, rent and utility bills, officials say some students have become charity cases. The electricity in one student's apartment was turned off after his bill reached $700.

"Churches and individuals in the community have been donating money, food and shelter, but this help is short-term," said John Enger, the school's public information director.

"The financial condition of Nigerian students in the United States is an embarrassment to all of us associated with international education," said Dixon Johnson of the University of Tennessee.

August 11, 1983, Rocky Mountain News, Denver, Co. Reprinted by permission.

Johnson, president of the National Association of Foreign Student Advisors, said one Nigerian student, a young woman who is blind, has not received a penny of her promised living expenses since arriving in Knoxville last March. He said university officials are using her $4,500 tuition deposit to pay for her room and board.

CRITERIA FOR REVOLUTION

REVOLUTIONS ARE MOST LIKELY TO OCCUR WHEN--

1. The country is governed by a dictator.

2. Individuals and groups feel that their civil rights have been violated.

3. There are conflicts based on race, language, ethnic differences, and religion.

4. There is a large gap between the rich and the poor.

5. There is competition for limited land or resources, and the economic system is seen by the poor to be unjust.

6. Foreign companies or governments are seen as exploiters--taking unfair advantage economically or politically.

7. The government is unable to act effectively because it does not have strong enough authority.

8. Natural disasters such as floods, earthquakes, and droughts have recently occurred.

9. There is a foreign invasion or other experience with foreign aggression.

10. Regions of the country have different economic and ethnic makeups, especially if one region controls the government.

COUNTRY CARDS

Country A

Country A is in Latin America. Most of the population lives in a narrow strip of irrigated land along the coast. The rest of the country is covered with high mountains or jungle. Almost half of the population is Indian, 30 percent of whom do not speak the national language. Over 90 percent are Roman Catholic.

Country A exports large quantities of fish. Agricultural products, including cotton and sugar, are raised on large plantations along the coast. Minerals-- copper, lead, molybdenum, silver, zinc, and iron--are found in the mountains. Oil has been discovered in the jungle and is being developed by foreign companies.

The government of Country A is a democracy. Economic problems include periodic food shortages, large foreign debts, and a high inflation rate (50 percent/yr.). Per capita annual income is $655. The richest 5 percent of the population makes 34 percent of the national income.

Literacy is 79 percent. Life expectancy is sixty of age.

The largest trading partners of Country A are the United States, European community, and Japan. Country A has had border conflicts with two of its neighboring countries, one of which turned into open warfare recently.

Country A- Roles

1. Wealthy factory owner
2. Illiterate Indian farmer in the mountains
3. Worker on coastal plantation
4. Foreign oil company executive
5. Indian who has moved from mountains to city--a manual laborer

Country B

Country B is in Asia. It is made up of a chain of islands, most of which are mountainous and heavily forested. A coastal plain on the largest island is the location of the capital city, and also the industrial and cultural center of the country. There are three official languages, and ninety others spoken by minorities in the rural areas. Most of the population is Roman Catholic, with a Muslim minority in the south.

Country B is still basically agricultural, but has recently made progress in developing industries such as food processing, clothing, paper, and electrical appliances. The government owns all natural resources. Serious floods were a problem until a series of dams were built by the government.

The government of Country B is a new democracy. Coup attempts by various groups still frequently occur.

Although the national income has risen because of the success of new industries, a high birth rate has tended to increase the gap between the rich and poor. Per capita income is $560. Unemployment is high. The richest 5 percent of the population makes 25 percent of the national income.

Literacy is 88 percent. Life expectancy is 63 years of age.

The United States maintains military bases in Country B, and is also one of the largest markets for its exports.

Country B- Roles

1. Muslim farmer in the south
2. Opposition political leader
3. Middle class shopkeeper in the capital city
4. Plantation owner
5. Small farmer in former flood area

© CTIR
University of Denver

Country C

Country C is in Asia. Most of its area is occupied by its capital city, which is also one of the largest ports in the world. There are four official languages and five major religions represented in its population. Fourteen percent of the population belongs to an ethnic minority with strong ties to a large neighboring country.

Most of the people make their living in trade and manufacturing. Major industries include shipbuilding, oil refining, electronics, banking, and textiles. Country C has one of the highest growth rates in the world.

The government of Country C is a democracy, but civil rights have been curtailed in recent years. The same man has led the country for over twenty years. Opposition to his rule is suppressed.

Per capita income is second in Asia at $7410. Unemployment is low, and inflation is lower than in the United States.

Country C has strong trade ties with Japan and the U.S., as well as with its large neighboring country.

Country C- Roles

1. Middle class bank employee
2. Construction worker from minority ethnic group
3. Textile factory owner
4. Electrical engineer
5. Opposition political leader

© CTIR
University of Denver

Country D

Country D is the largest country in Africa. The northern part of the country is desert, with a fertile river valley. The central and southern parts are plains that have plentiful rain and rich soil. There are two major ethnic groups in the north (including Arabs), and numerous tribal groups in the south. Arabic, the official language, is spoken by 51 percent of the population. There are thirty-two other languages spoken. The population is primarily Muslim, 25 percent traditional (tribal) and 5 percent Christian.

Most of the people (over 85 percent) make their living in agriculture. Agricultural products such as cotton, sesame, peanuts, and gum arabic are Country D's principal exports. Although Country D is considered one of the most promising agricultural areas in the world, the economy has suffered from drought and a high inflation rate (over 25 percent).

The government of Country D was put into power by a military coup. It is dominated by the Arab-Muslim part of the population. A limited amount of self-government has been granted to the southern region. Country D has had close ties with the Soviet Union, but recently these ties have weakened and it has moved closer to the United States. There have been several attempted coups to take over the government, including a communist group, and one supported by Libya.

Per capita income is $320. The richest 5 percent of the population makes 21 percent of the national income.

Literacy in Country D is 20 percent. Life expectancy is 48 years.

Country D- Roles

1. Arab farmer in the northern river valley
2. Military officer
3. Worker on peanut farm
4. Agricultural development worker
5. Owner of large cotton farm

113   © CTIR
                                    University of Denver

Country E

Country E is a small Latin American country. The central highlands contain high volcanic mountains. Narrow coastal plains and river valleys are densely populated, and there is very little agricultural land per capita. Over half the population is Indian. Most speak Spanish, with some Indian dialects spoken in the mountains. The population is 90 percent Roman Catholic.

Country E depends heavily on coffee exports, as well as sugar and bananas, most of which are grown on large plantations. Multinational corporations and wealthy families control much of the land. The richest 5 percent of the people makes over half of the national income. Per capita income is $930.

The government of Country E is controlled by the upper class and the military. There has been sporadic political violence for the past thirty years. In 1975, a group called the Guerrilla Army of the Poor was founded, which has been supported by many Indians.

Literacy is 48 percent. Life expectancy is 61 years. Because of a high birth rate, the population of Country D is expected to double in less than twenty-five years.

The United States has actively supported the government of Country E, in spite of its poor record on human rights. Members of the Roman Catholic Church have become involved in publicizing the situation in Country E in the United States.

Country E- Roles

1. Illiterate Indian peasant in highlands
2. Wealthy coffee plantation owner
3. Military officer
4. Local priest
5. Middle class student

© CTIR
University of Denver

Country F

Country F is an African country twice the size of California. The center of the country is a hot dry plateau, with lakes to the west, more temperate highlands in the north and south, and a narrow coastal plain. There are over one hundred thirty tribal groups in Country F, with a mixture of Europeans, Arabs, and Asians on the coasts. The official languages are Swahili and English. Thirty percent of the population is Muslim, 30 percent Christian, and 40 percent follow traditional tribal religions.

Over 90 percent of Country F's economy is agricultural. The major crops are sisal, cotton, coffee, and tea. Minerals, including diamonds, gold, and salt, are being mined in limited quantities.

The government of Country F is socialist. The same man has been in power since 1964 and is considered one of Africa's leading statesmen. Banks and many industries are owned by the government. Approximately half the population lives in cooperative farming villages. Per capita income is $250.

Literacy is 85 percent. Life expectancy is 52 years.

Country F received aid from China and has maintained a neutral position between the Soviet Union and the United States.

Country F- Roles

1. Member of small tribal group in rural area
2. Government worker in capital city
3. Farm worker living in cooperative village
4. Muslim Arab shopkeeper
5. Worker in government factory

ROLES

ELITES

    Banker - United States
    Banker - Mexico
    Factory Owner - Japan
    Factory Owner - Thailand
    Plantation Owner - Brazil
    Plantation Owner - Chad
    President - Nigeria
    Prime Minister - India
    Network Reporter - Canada
    Electronics Engineer - Western Europe
    Secretary of Transportation - Soviet Union
    Olympic Coach - Romania

COMMONERS

    Factory Worker - Mexico
    Factory Worker - Western Europe
    Factory Worker - India
    Fisherman - Brazil
    Fisherman - Soviet Union
    Fisherman - Thailand
    Store Clerk - United States
    School Teacher - Japan
    Housewife - Canada
    Bus Driver - Brazil
    Soldier - Nigeria
    Beggar - India
    Oil Rigger - Mexico
    Bar Owner - United States
    Taxi Driver - Romania
    Farmer - Chad
    Farmer - India

GALTUNG'S WEB: TRUE-FALSE TEST

Mark the following statements "true" if they are likely to happen, or "false" if they are not likely to happen.

		TRUE	FALSE
1.	The Queen of England visits the President of the U.S.	___	___
2.	A Canadian exporter sells natural gas to a Japanese importer.	___	___
3.	An American gas station attendant meets a Chinese farmer.	___	___
4.	Canadian and Swedish scientists experiment about acid rain.	___	___
5.	An Ethiopian nomad talks with a Thai dockworker.	___	___
6.	A Curtis-Mathes TV company owner sells American TVs to a Nigerian TV distributor.	___	___
7.	A student from Moscow exchanges places with a student from East Berlin, both of whose parents are party members.	___	___
8.	A Paraguayan street thief chats with an unemployed Detroit auto worker.	___	___
9.	A Japanese shipbuilder buys timber from a Brazilian commercial farmer.	___	___
10.	A Chad student studies in New York, and a professor convences him to stay in the United States.	___	___
11.	A French boutique owner buys handcrafted silk from a Thai silk manufacturer.	___	___
12.	The owner of a West German McDonald's chain buys beef from a big Montana rancher.	___	___
13.	Korean fisherman talks about lures with a British doctor who fishes on weekends.	___	___
14.	A U.S. banker schedules a loan for a Mexican banker.	___	___

© CTIR
University of Denver

15. A French scientist teaches nuclear technology to an
     Indian scientist in order to develop weapons.   ____   ____

16. A British museum curator visits the Cultural Minister
     in Beijing to arrange a Chinese art exhibit in London.   ____   ____

17. An Argentinian communications manager agrees to let
     Calvin Klein company place ads on Argentine TV.   ____   ____

18. A U.S. soldier plays cards with an East German boy.   ____   ____

19. United States and Japanese trade representatives
     meet in Tokyo to discuss tariffs.   ____   ____

20. A Swiss doctor persuades a Kenyan hospital director
     to give bottled formula to newborn babies, instead
     of breast milk.   ____   ____

DESIGNS

1.

Nancy Kuo, Chinese Paper-cut Pictures, 1964. Reprinted by permission.

2.

3.

4.

5.

121

6.

7.

8.

9.

10.

123

11.

12.

13.

14.

15.

PAPERCUTS INFORMATION SHEET

For each of the papercuts, list clues about Chinese culture and values reflected by that design. Note the dates when each papercut was made.

1. Traditional _____

_____

2. 1980 _____

_____

3. 1980 _____

_____

4. 1973 _____

_____

5. 1973 _____

_____

6. Sixth Century _____

_____

7. 1973 _____

_____

8. 1973 _____

_____

9. 1980 _____

_____

10. 1980 _____

_____

11. 1980 _____

_____

12. 1973 _____

_____

13. Traditional _____

_____

14. Traditional _____

_____

15. Traditional _____

_____

What conclusions can you make about changes in China based on an examination of the papercuts? _____

_____

_____

List examples of Western art that also reflect cultural changes (paintings, films, folktales, etc). Be specific. _____

_____

_____

What kinds of art in your culture are similar to papercuts as an inexpensive form of popular folk art? _____

_____

_____

If you have studied other world cultures, what forms of folk art also reflect cultural change? Give examples. _____

_____

_____

RULES FOR CHINESE STUDENTS*

1. Love the motherland, the people and the Communist Party. Study well and make progress every day.

2. Go to school on time, and do not be absent without reason. Listen attentively to teaching and finish your homework.

3. Adhere to physical training. Take an active part in after school activities.

4. Pay attention to personal hygiene. Dress neatly and do not spit on the floor.

5. Love labor and do everything you can.

6. Lead a simple life, waste no food, do not be picky with food or clothing, and do not spend money foolishly.

7. Observe school discipline and public order.

8. Respect teachers and older people. Unite with your classmates. Be polite. Do not scold or fight with other students.

9. Take care of the interests of the collective and watch out for public property.

10. Be honest and brave. Correct mistakes wherever they are found.

_____

Translated from the Chinese by Wong Ku-hiang, March 1983.

POPULATION PYRAMID—CHINA

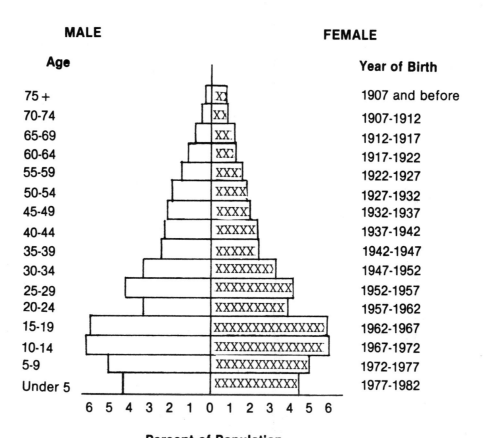

MALE		FEMALE
Age		Year of Birth
75+		1907 and before
70-74		1907-1912
65-69		1912-1917
60-64		1917-1922
55-59		1922-1927
50-54		1927-1932
45-49		1932-1937
40-44		1937-1942
35-39		1942-1947
30-34		1947-1952
25-29		1952-1957
20-24		1957-1962
15-19		1962-1967
10-14		1967-1972
5-9		1972-1977
Under 5		1977-1982

6 5 4 3 2 1 0 1 2 3 4 5 6

Percent of Population

Figures for this chart were taken from CIA, National Foreign Assessment
Center, China: Economic Indicators (ER-78, 10750, Dec. 1978), p. 9.

POPULATION PYRAMID—UNITED STATES

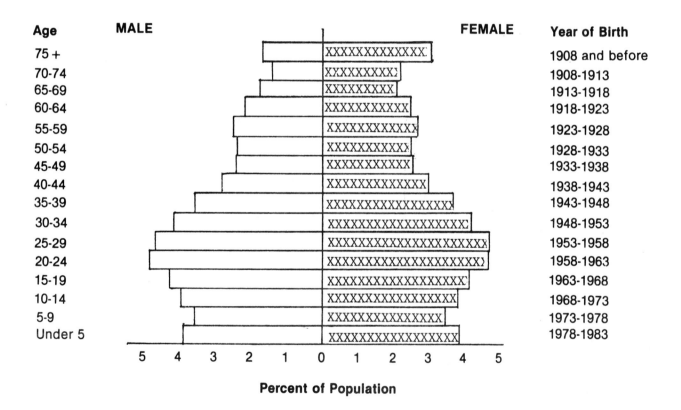

Percent of Population

Figures for this chart are from the U.S. Bureau of the Census, 1980 Census of the Population.

POPULATION PYRAMID-QUESTIONNAIRE

A. To answer these questions, refer to the Chinese population pyramid on Handout #11.

1. What age group contains the largest percentage of individuals?   _____

2. Are there more males or more females in this age group?   _____

3. What is the percentage of the population 65 years or older?   _____

4. How many Chinese are there between the ages of 10 and 19?   _____

5. How does this compare with the total U.S. population?   _____

    _____

6. Approximately 50 percent of China's population is below what age?   _____

7. China's birth rate has dropped from 45.4 percent in 1949 to 10.8 percent today. In light of this fact, why is there still such a large age group below the age of 20?   _____

    _____

8. What reasons might there be for larger numbers of males in most age groups?   _____

    _____

132

B. Compare the population pyramids of China and the United States. List below at least five significant differences between the two. For each difference, list at least one way in which it has an impact on culture.

      Difference   Cultural Impact

1. _____   1. _____

   _____   _____

2. _____   2. _____

   _____   _____

3. _____   3. _____

   _____   _____

4. _____   4. _____

   _____   _____

5. _____   5. _____

   _____   _____

6. _____   6. _____

   _____   _____

7. _____   7. _____

   _____   _____

C. You are a member of a planning commission for the Chinese government. What problems would you predict for China in the next twenty years based on your analysis of the population pyramid? (Example: China has a larger proportion of its population under the age of twenty than the U.S., and there will be a need for an increasing number of jobs as these individuals reach maturity.)

Economic Problems _____

_____

_____

_____

_____

_____

Political Problems: _____

_____

_____

_____

_____

_____

Social Problems: _____

_____

_____

_____

_____

_____

WHO CAN I TURN TO?

Imagine that you or a member of your family is faced with each of the problems listed below. In the blank after each problem, name the person, group, or institution to whom you would most likely turn for help. You can list more than one.

Your bicycle is stolen from your garage. _____

_____

You need someone to care for your 2-year-old while you are at work.

_____

You are a housewife with no particular job skills and you want to go back to work. _____

_____

Your father is physically abusing your mother and your brother. _____

_____

Someone moves in across the street and starts giving loud parties late into the night. _____

Your baby needs to have a shot. _____

A group of teenagers in the neighborhood are hanging out at the corner store because they cannot get jobs and don't have anything to do. _____

_____

There is an empty lot in the neighborhood with litter, bottles, and weeds.

_____

An elderly widow lives down the street from you and sits alone on her porch most of the time. _____

You feel that public transportation to your neighborhood is not adequate and would like to complain to higher authorities. _____

_____

THE NEIGHBORHOOD COMMITTEE

Your class is acting as a neighborhood committee in China. Today's meeting has been called to deal with three typical problems. For each problem:

1. Listen to each participant's account of the problem.

2. Explore a variety of possible solutions, including the advantages and disadvantages of each solution for the group as well as for the individuals concerned.

3. Decide on appropriate action, referring the problem to other authorities if necessary.

NOTE: As you discuss each case, try to take a Chinese perspective and consider the nature of present-day Chinese society and its economy.

THREE CASES

<u>PROBLEM A</u>

Some of the neighborhood's senior middle school (high school) graduates this year have not been able to find jobs. A group of about five to ten young men have been hanging out at the local small grocery store. The owner of the store has complained to the neighborhood committee because he says that the teenagers create a bad impression and harrass his customers. Several of the boys have been asked to attend this meeting along with the store owner to discuss the problem.

<u>NOTE</u>: Facts about the Chinese economy which apply to this case.

Although small stores can now be individually owned, they must be run by a family or a cooperative. No one may hire another person to work for him.

Jobs are assigned to middle school graduates by the government; they do not apply at factories or stores themselves.

ROLES: Store owner
        Three teenage boys

PROBLEM B

One of the families in the neighborhood is considering divorce. Both of the parents work--the father as a technician in a steel factory, and the mother as a crane operator in the same factory. There are two children, one two-year-old, and one four-year-old. Because both the husband and wife come from other parts of the country, they rarely see their families. Their two-room apartment is part of a large traditional home built around a courtyard, now housing five families. The husband brought the case to the neighborhood committee because his wife told him that she wanted a divorce. She complained that her husband expects her to do all the housework even though her job at the factory is physically demanding. In addition, she must spend an hour each day taking the children to their day care center and picking them up. Physically exhausted each day, she has become irritable and they have had some serious arguments. He accuses her of not being a good wife and mother, and she threatens to return home to the countryside to live with her family, where she could get help with the children and the chores. The director of the day care center has reported that the four-year-old daughter is showing signs of withdrawal, possibly related to the constant arguments she hears at home. Both husband and wife, several other residents of the courtyard, and the director of the day care center are present at this meeting.

NOTE: Facts about Chinese society which apply to this case.

Divorce is very rare in China. Many who have been divorced have had difficulty remarrying because of prejudice against divorced individuals.

Attitudes about men's and women's roles are changing, but housework is still primarily considered the woman's responsibility.

ROLES: Husband
Wife
Director of the Day Care Center
Three other residents of the courtyard

© CTIR
University of Denver

PROBLEM C

There are a growing number of retired people in the neighborhood who have lived there all their lives and have had difficulty adjusting to the changes around them. Some of them have no family close by. Their sons and daughters have either moved to other parts of the country, emigrated, or died as a result of war or disease. They receive 70 percent of their former salary, as well as other benefits such as free health care, which help make them financially secure. However, many of them, particularly the women, cannot read or write and have little to do during the day. Many have chronic health problems that must be checked frequently by medical personnel. Others are retired workers and professionals with valuable skills in the areas of crafts, carpentry, and foreign languages. Because the large Chinese extended family is no longer available for this older generation, they don't feel useful and a part of the community. Several members of the neighborhood committee have been concerned with the problems faced by retired people and have invited representatives to this meeting to discuss possible ways in which the committee could help.

ROLES: A male retired worker, 70 years old, former carpenter
A female, 75 years old, skilled in embroidery, active, and in good health
A male, 65 years old, former English teacher
A female, 62 years old, raised eight children, never worked
A male, 68 years old, retired army officer, fought in Chinese Revolution
A female, 61 years old, retired jade factory worker, carved jade into flowers and animals

139

CHINESE STATISTICS

Composition of Chinese Labor Force:

Sector	1957 Number of Workers in Millions	1957 Percent of Total	1989 Number of Workers in Millions	1989 Percent of Total
Agriculture	231.53	84.5	379.62	74.5
Manufacturing and Services	42.47	15.5	133.38	25.5

Per Capita Income:

Area	1977	1985	Percent Increase
Rural	65.4 Yuan*	397.6 Yuan	100+
Urban	411.5 Yuan	569.9 Yuan	38.5

Ratio of Urban: Rural Per Capita Income:	1977	1980
	6.3:1	4.8:1

Rural Caloric Intake Per Capita: 1977-1981 Increased 16.8 percent

Total Value of Chinese Agricultural Output: 1977-1981 Increased 17.9 percent

Urban Unemployment 1979: Approximately 20 million (20 percent of urban population)

*Chinese Yuan in 1989 was worth approximately $3.71 U.S.

Source: Chinese Government Statistics, 1982 Census.

© CTIR
University of Denver

CASE STUDY

Mei Xiao-lan is a twenty-year-old member of a rural commune in South China, about thirty miles from the large city of Guangzhou.* She and her brother and sister spend much of their time working in the fields, tending their family's private plot, and taking care of the pigs and ducks that the family sells in the free market.** Because there are five members of the family who are working, the Mei family is considered more prosperous than some of their neighbors, with a yearly income of 800 Yuan (approximately $400 U.S.).

Xiao-lan has completed junior middle school (equivalent to an American junior high school), which is as far as most rural students go. Her parents wanted her to go to work so that the family income would increase. Sometimes she envies her cousin in the city who is studying science in senior middle school, although she knows that her cousin may have to wait one or two years for a job after she graduates.

The Mei family is proud of their achievements in the past few years. Because they are close to the city, they can sell some of the vegetables, pigs, and ducks they raise there. This gives them a higher income than peasants in more remote areas. The family income has doubled in the past five years. Much of what they made has been invested in more animals, which in turn led to greater profits. Since the end of the Cultural Revolution in China, such "capitalism" by individual peasants is no longer frowned upon by the government, and they have been encouraged to expand their sideline activities.

This has not been without cost, however. More work means longer hours, sometimes up to ten to twelve hours per day, seven days a week during the busy season. In hot, humid south China, tasks such as planting rice seedlings in the flooded paddies can mean backbreaking work. Xiao-lan often thinks how much nicer it would be to have a factory job with regular hours in the city.

The family eats well, probably better than their city cousins who often cannot get much of a variety of fresh vegetables. Xiao-lan remembers the leaner years, when the family had meat only on special occasions and the grain allocations were lower per family. Now, because they are raising their own animals, the family eats meat or poultry several times per week.

Xiao-lan's sister, who is eighteen, suffers from diabetes. She has difficulty getting medicine and must make the trip to the city several times a year to see a specialist, since none of the health workers in the commune are trained in this speciality.

---

* Guangzhou - Canton
** Free Market - Place where peasants sell goods for their own profit, in contrast to the cooperative and government-operated markets.

In the evenings, Xiao-lan and her friends like to watch the family's TV, which they bought last year with some of their savings. It makes them feel closer to the life in cities such as Beijing, Shanghai, and Guangzhou, although it also reminds them how much fun it would be to be able to go to the movies or the theater in the city.

Next month Xiao-lan's cousin will come for a visit. It is the busy season on the commune, and the family will welcome an extra hand to work in the fields. Her cousin enjoys getting away from the heat and pollution of Guangzhou. She especially enjoys the Mei family's spacious home, which she says is much better than her family's cramped two-room apartment. Her parents cannot join her because as factory workers they do not get vacations except for a few national holidays.

Mei Xiao-lan thinks of her life on the farm as unglamorous, although she has a certain amount of economic security. She worries what will happen if next year the weather is bad or the government changes its policies. Will she marry a peasant and spend the rest of her life on the commune? Sometimes she wonders what her life would be like if she could trade places with her city cousin.

ALTERNATIVE PROGRAMS

Youth to the Countryside

In this program, millions of middle school (high school) graduates were sent to rural areas to help counterbalance the increase in urban population. Many of them were sent to frontier provinces, where they helped in education and health programs as well as working in the fields. Because the growing number of middle school graduates had been a major cause of unemployment in the cities, this program helped to reduce the unemployment rate. The students had valuable skills to offer the peasants, who in turn taught them a very different style of life from that of the cities. Students gained greater respect for the peasants by actually taking part in farm labor and talking with them about the hardships of their life. Some students said that the experience gave them a greater appreciation for the many different ethnic and social groups that make up their country. They had a feeling of being an important part of "building socialism" in China, of helping the nation to develop. (United States' students might compare some of the positive aspects of this program to the Peace Corps or similar domestic volunteer programs, although the Chinese students were by no means volunteers.) When the program was at its height, over two million urban youth were sent to the countryside each year. Many were unsure when, or if, they would be allowed to return to the city.

Commune Workshops

The basic idea of this program was to introduce industry into the rural areas; to give the peasants an understanding of what was involved in the manufacturing process and involve them in the national development effort. It was also thought that the program would make use of extra workers in the rural areas, increase peasant income, and prevent further migration to urban areas. Some of the original projects were quite ambitious. The most famous were the "backyard steel furnaces," primitive attempts to have peasants produce small quantities of steel. Most of these were abandoned within a few years. However, a number of other kinds of workshops were introduced that did succeed in adding to commune income and providing needed products. For example, one commune had a peanut oil factory, brick kiln, furniture shop, and herbal medicine workshop. Peasants were trained to repair farm machinery and bicycles. Although the number of workers involved was a small percentage of the commune's population, this program was thought to give peasants a more active role in national development and to make them more self-reliant.

Responsibility System (Ziren zhi)

The basic idea of the Responsibility System is that peasant earnings are directly linked to output. Each family signs a contract to deliver part of what they produce to the state. They may keep whatever they produce above this quota or sell it at higher prices to the state. Under this system, collective labor as it was known before does not really exist. A family that works harder and produces more, even though they do it on government-owned land, receives a higher income. Some families have begun to specialize in certain crops, especially those near urban areas who can get high prices for poultry, tobacco, and other products. With their new profits, peasants are buying consumer products such as bicycles, tape recorders, and television sets. Some are building new homes. The agricultural output nationwide exhibited a marked increase in the first three years of the program, but there was concern that inequities, both within communes and among regions, would widen. Wealthy regions and families with many active workers would prosper, while more remote and infertile regions, and families with fewer resources would find their position deteriorating. Critics asked what had become of the old socialist maxim, "From each according to his ability. To each according to his need."

Urban Identification Booklet (Hukou System)

A hukou is a small paper booklet in which members of each urban household are registered. Without a hukou, one cannot receive food rations, a job, or housing. Before a peasant can move to the city (or a youth sent to the countryside return to the city), he or she must first receive a hukou from the government. During the 1970s this was very difficult to accomplish. Periodic checks of urban neighborhoods by neighborhood committee officials or police still locate peasants without hukou who are subsequently ordered to return to their communes. Through this system, China has been able to avoid the problem of having large numbers of unemployed peasants flock to the cities, as happened in Cairo and Calcutta.

THE JAPANESE FAMILY

Within the Japanese family, the father is treated in many ways as a high-status guest in the home. A welcome, friendly, and even jovial guest, but one who stands on the periphery of the intimate circle of mother and children.

One woman, for example, explained that she dislikes Sundays because her husband is home the whole day and consequently she and the children cannot relax. Another woman confessed that it is better for the father to come home a little late and eat supper separately because when he is home the children must be more restrained. They cannot talk, bustle around, and enjoy the supper hour when the father is at home. Another lady who suffers from psychosomatic difficulties has a husband who does some traveling as part of his work; her difficulties become worse when he is stationed at the home office and comes home early every night.

The coalition of mother and children is not necessarily hostile to the father. It may mean only that the mother and children share things that are not shared with the father, and that they see themselves as united for common objectives which are different from those of the father.

The basic alignment is manifested in many ways. The wife and children are reserved in the presence of the father. They keep secrets from him, and plot to deal with him. They are to some extent on perpetual good behavior when the father is present. Like American students with their professors, they may joke and talk freely with fathers about many topics, but relax more freely and tell other kinds of jokes in his absence.

The separateness between father and family is accentuated by the amount of time the mother and children spend together without the father. In comparison with the American middle-class family, the Japanese mother spends more time with the children, the father less time. Because the wife and children virtually center their world in the home, they have an intensely close relationship that is essentially impossible for the father to share.

The father's power also contributes to the emotional distance between him and the rest of the family. Because the wife and children know that the father may become firm or demanding, they are cautious, reserved, and rarely completely at ease in his presence.

From Ezra F. Vogel, Japans New Middle Class (Berkeley: University of California Press, 1961) pp 208-16. Reprinted with permission.
(See also The Japanese Mind, by Robert Christopher, NY: Ballantyne Books, 1983, pp 64-79.)

145

Part of the reason that the relationship between the father and the rest of the family is so stable, though, is that difficulties can be contained without disrupting the basic pattern of relationships. If, as with many modern young couples, the husband and wife desire to be closer, this is possible. But if there are difficulties and the father is disappointed with the mother and the children, he can simply enjoy the pleasures of the bars and his colleagues from his company, and spend less time at home.

Similarly, because the wife ordinarily expects to get much of her emotional comfort and support from her children and intimate friends, she is not so disappointed if she and her husband do not have an intimate relationship.

APARTO FLOOR PLAN

Entire floor plan is 6.2 meters long x 4.6 meters wide.

1 tatami mat = 90 cm. x 180 cm.

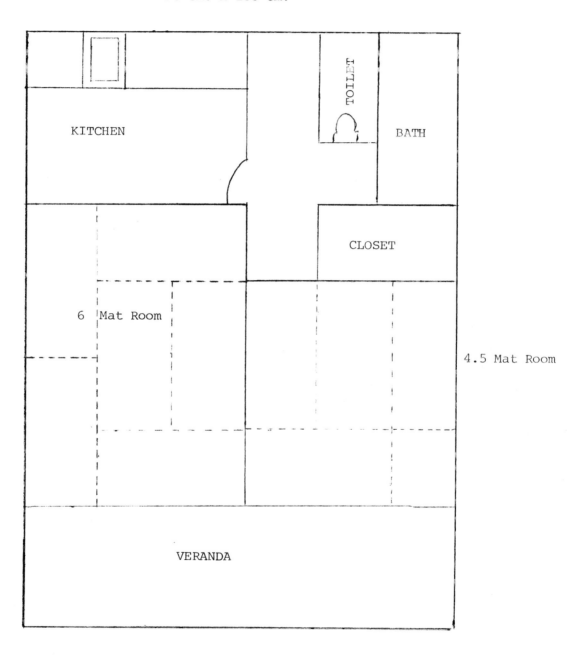

APARTO FURNISHINGS

4 chairs 1 m. x 1 m.   linens

kotatsu 2 m. x 2 m.   records

4 futons (beds) 1 futon = 2 m. x 1 m.   books

television set   bookcase

water heater   dishes

kitchen table 1 1/2 m. x 1/2 m.   bathtub

4 chests of drawers 1 m. x 1/2 m.   bathroom rug

artificial closet   1/2 .x 1/2 m. x 1 1/2 m.   calendar

rice cooker   photo album

stove 1 m. x 1/2 m.   souvenirs

Washer and dryer 1 m. x 1/2 m.

space heater

stereo

radio

electric fan

3 lamps

4 zabuton (pillows)

pictures

refrigerator 1/2 m. x 1/2 m. x 1 1/2 m.

fishbowl

toys

towels

U.S. WOMAN BATTLES JAPAN ALIEN POLICY

In a tiny courtroom devoid of adornment, testimony has droned on for months in the trial of an American woman whose offense was to refuse to press her left index finger on an ink pad.

Court sessions are conducted only sporadically, and perhaps a dozen spectators show up, some drifting off to sleep in the thick air of Yokohama District Court.

Despite the lack of high drama, those in the courtroom are witnessing a key challenge, one of the few so far, to a law that requires every foreigner living in Japan to report to the authorities and submit to fingerprinting of the left index finger every few years.

Not many democratic countries insist on this sort of regular scrutiny of foreigners. The United States, for instance, fingerprints only those people from abroad seeking permanent resident status, and does it only once.

Japan, however, likes to keep a closer check, reflecting an us-and-them attitude toward strangers that is deeply rooted in the nation's history.

Only 800,000 foreigners live in Japan, less than seven-tenths of 1 percent of the population of 118 million. Of these, all but 80,000 come from Japan's closest neighbors, North and South Korea, and China.

For Westerners, in particular, their status is reinforced by the word used for them -- "gaijin" -- which means "outside person," and it is a term not without pejorative connotations.

One day in September, Kathleen Morikawa, an American teacher of English who is married to a Japanese university lecturer, went to the city office in Yamato, not far from Yokohama, to fill out the necessary forms under the Alien Registration Law.

The law, which goes back 31 years and has been revised several times, requires foreigners above the age of 16 who intend to live in Japan for more than a year, to register with local authorities every five years. They must also be fingerprinted.

Japanese a People Apart

The fingerprinting controversy touches on a broader issue of how the Japanese define themselves as a people apart from all others.

Ezra F. Vogel, Japans New Middle Class (Berkeley: University of California Press, 1961) pp 208-216. Reprinted with permission.

For example, the children of Japanese businessmen and government workers who have spent years abroad are routinely sent to special schools designed to reintroduce them to their society and its ways.

Similarly, a computer specialist born of Japanese parents and brought up in the United States moved to Tokyo but found the adjustment less than smooth. He has come to realize, he said, that "I will never be accepted as a Japanese."

Legally, the question of who is or is not a Japanese arises in several ways. One that causes controversy is the "Nationality Law."

Under this 33-year-old statute, a child must have a Japanese father to achieve Japanese citizenship; the only exceptions are for cases in which the youngster is illegitimate or the father is unknown.

As a result, children born to a Japanese woman and a non-Japanese man are registered as aliens at birth, placing them at a social, and sometimes a legal, disadvantage.

Efforts are now under way to amend the law to remove its discriminatory aspects, and changes seem likely soon.

In addition, some local governments, including Kanagawa Prefecture, where Mrs. Morikawa is on trial, have asked the national authorities to change the Alien Registration Law, at least by dropping the fingerprint requirement.

Treating Her Like a Criminal

Mrs. Morikawa, 33, who has been living in Japan for 10 years and has gone through the process several times, decided this time that she would object.

It was treating her like a criminal, she said. The only Japanese forced to do the same were those accused of crimes. In fact, Mrs. Morikawa pointed out, "unless a warrant for their arrest is issued, Japanese criminal suspects do not have to be fingerprinted--they must give their permission first."

What made the case unusual was that in February the Yokohama public prosecutor indicted her. In all, some 30 foreigners have refused to be fingerprinted, nearly all of them Koreans who are officially considered to be aliens even though many were born in Japan.

Thus far, the Pittsburgh-born Mrs. Morikawa is one of the few to stand trial. If convicted, she could receive up to a year in jail and an $800 fine.

150

"In order to control aliens coming into this sovereign territory, we need some identification system," said Nobuyoshi Kamei, a Justice Ministry official in charge of the program. Fingerprints are needed, Kamei said, because photo identification alone is ineffective.

Critics have charged that the system is really designed to monitor the 670,000 Koreans in this country. Many, perhaps most, are the children and grandchildren of Koreans brought to Japan for forced labor in World War II.

Naturalization laws are written in such a way that it is difficult for these second- and third-generation Koreans to obtain Japanese citizenship. The process requires them, among other things, to give up their Korean names for official purposes.

I San Ho, a 26-year-old Korean who runs a kindergarten in the city of Kawasaki, refused to be fingerprinted last August after going along with the system for years.

"I want to live in this society as a Korean," he said, although he acknowledged that "since I was born in Japan, grew up in Japan and went to Japanese schools, my lifestyle is completely Japanese."

A HARD DAY'S NIGHT

A Hard Day's Night

As soon as Kotaro Nohmura, an executive director of Taiyo Kogyo, an Osaka tent manufacturer, arrives home from work at nearly midnight, he looks in on his four children. They are asleep, just as they were when he left for work at 7:30 that morning. A few fond glances are usually the only contact Nohmura, 37, has with his two sons (7 and 4 months) and two daughters (5 and 9) during the week. Like most Japanese executives, his day starts early and ends only after a long night of business entertaining.

Nohmura earns $51,000 a year before taxes, which enables him to house his family in a four-room apartment in the outskirts of Kobe, a port city. Six days a week, he gets up at 7 and eats a Western-style breakfast prepared by his 32-year-old wife Sanae. Then he is out the door and into a Toyota Crown sedan, which he drives 40 minutes to his company's head office in a bustling section of Osaka (pop. 2.6 million).

Each Monday morning at 8:30, Nohmura and 100 co-workers assemble for *chokai*, a corporate pep rally, where they kick off the week by reciting twelve company creeds. (No. 7: "Once you've grabbed hold of a potential piece of business, never let it go, no matter what—even at the risk of your own life.") One piece of business that Nohmura is grabbing involves the $4 billion science and technology fair in Tsukuba in 1985. It will be needing giant ents to accommodate sightseers.

The young executive is driven not only by his country's competitive culture but also by family ties. His father is the founder and chairman of the company, which had revenues last year of $106 million. "If I failed to do as well as or better than the rest of the people in the company, I would end up a laughingstock as an executive," he says.

Nohmura spends most of his mornings at his desk in a

MASACHIKA SUHARA

Kotaro Nohmura in his cubbyhole office in Osaka

cubbyhole office. He likes his small space, saying, "I can get almost everything I need without having to stand up every time." There he writes reports and discusses new tent designs with engineers. The executive almost never goes to business lunches, preferring a quick snack of a bowl of noodles at a nearby restaurant. He spends the afternoon making the rounds of local customers and inspecting tents being constructed. Then he calls it a day at about 5:30.

But Nohmura's work is far from finished. On a typical recent evening he first went to a meeting of the Osaka Jaycees, where he serves as vice chairman. He and fellow Jaycees discussed the national elections with a writer from an Osaka newspaper. The group's conclusion: more support was needed for conservative legislators. Nohmura says, "I love these kinds of meetings. Politics, after all, is bound to have an impact on business."

After the Jaycees' session, Nohmura went on to his evening's business entertainment. He escorted a favored client and one of the client's associates to an elegant restaurant ($110 a person) where, seated on cushions on a *tatami*-covered floor, they dined on a twelve-course meal that included clear soup, sashimi and tempura. That contrasted with the group's next stop, a Western-style nightspot, where Cardin-clad hostesses poured liberal amounts of whisky and brandy. Cost for the after-dinner stop, which continued until well after 11 p.m., was $360. "I don't like entertaining," says Nohmura, "but it has become an institution. If you persist in being a reformer, you would go to pieces in business. That, naturally, is something I have to avoid—no matter what."

When Nohmura returned home, his wife greeted him at the door. Then over a quiet cup of green tea, the couple talked about the coming Sunday, when the whole family would be going out to the beach for a picnic. Sunday will constitute Nohmura's one day off.

Reprinted with permission from Time, 8/1/83.

WE JAPANESE

In our personal relations with people outside our families we Japanese follow somewhat the same pattern as inside our families. We have what are called the oyabun-kobun relationships, which are like father-son relationships, all through our business world, in the political habatsu (factions), the bureaucracy, and in labor. The oya is the senior, the ko is the junior. My oya is the head of my department who went to Keio University many years before I did and who has taken an interest in me ever since I entered the company. Three of my classmates entered at the same time, and we have all become his ko. As our oya, he looks after our general welfare in all sorts of things. When I have personal problems or financial difficulties I always seek his advice. One time Akiko and I had a bad disagreement, which was surprising as she usually does as I ask her, and I went to my oya for his advice. He was very busy that day but listened to me for an hour and suggested what I should do. Then he called up Akiko on some pretext and talked with her. He didn't say anything about the disagreement, but told her how well I was doing in the company and that he knew she was a great help to me in making a happy home so that I could concentrate on my work and things like that. Anyway, we soon resolved the argument. He also arranged for my son to get into a particularly good school. The boy had passed the examination but we were afraid that others with better connections would fill all the places. My oya, however, knows the headmaster and was able to persuade him. I, of course, pay great respect to my oya and listen to him carefully and do as he says diligently. I do anything I can to increase his prestige by my good performance and attitude.

The oyabun-kobun relationship doesn't break even if I am transferred to another department. Several years ago, I was shifted from accounting into the economic research department for a year to help them and to gain wider experience, which is useful for the company. But I retained my ties to my oya in the accounting department, too. I would find a reason to visit his office every week or ten days to tell him what I was doing and to listen to his advice.

The oyabun-kobun goes all the way up and down. My oya is ko to the president of the company, who is a close friend of my oya's father. I am not so senior yet, but about a year ago some new men came into our department and two young Keio graduates were assigned to me as assistants. I have become their oya and am beginning to help them as best I can. I spend a lot of time making sure that I fulfill my oyabun-kobun obligations. But I feel very secure in the system. I think, too, all these oyabun-kobun relationships, which overlap, help to make our company stronger in personal relations and therefore to work better.

From Richard Halloran, Japan: Images and Realities (Tokyo: Tuttle, 1970), pp. 228-251. Reprinted with permission.

We Japanese are intensely competitive outside our families and small groups. We strive very hard for prestige and position, power and money, and even for space in our crowded country. But we are aware that excessive competition can be dangerous and could cause much harm in politics and business or daily life, if we did not control it. We have many ways of making sure that competition does not become too strong. My foreign friends, particularly one who is an aggressive American business man, says we control competition so much that we have none at all.

IBM: THE COLOSSUS THAT WORKS

IBM's strong corporate culture is the lengthened shadow of Thomas Watson Sr., a charismatic executive who joined the Computing-Tabulating-Recording Corp. in 1914, renamed it International Business Machines in 1924, and ran it until a month before his death in 1956. Watson was a visionary who believed above all in his company.

Under Watson, IBM had rules for practically everything. Employees were told what to wear (dark business suits, white shirts and striped ties) and what to drink (no alcohol, even when off the job), and were urged in signs posted everywhere to THINK. Aspiring executives usually started out in sales and marketing and were transferred so frequently that they took to joking that IBM stood for "I've Been Moved." Observes Gideon Gartner, chairman of the Gartner Group, a computer-research firm: "If you understand the Marines, you can understand IBM."

Many of the Watson-instilled codes remain in effect today, though in a softened form. All IBMers are subject to a 32-page code of business ethics. Sample warning from the blue-covered rulebook: "if IBM is about to build a new facility, you must not invest in land or business near the new site."

IBM salesmen can now drink at lunch, but if they do they are warned not to make further business calls that day. Male IBMers, who make up 80% of the 8,500 member sales force, must wear suits and ties when meeting prospective customers, although their shirts no longer must be white. Still, a neat and conservative appearance remains the IBM style. "I don't think I've ever seen an IBMer in a pink shirt or an outlandish tie," says Joseph Levy, a vice president for International Data, a Massachusetts-based computer market-research firm. The THINK signs have largely vanished, but the old admonition remains the title of the company's employee magazine.

IBM has combined Watson's stern codes with a deep and genuine concern for the welfare of employees, who number 215,000 in the U.S. with an additional 150,000 abroad. The company has often fired workers, but it has never laid anyone off to cut costs; instead it retrains and reassigns them. The company's salaries and perks are widely regarded as among the most attractive in the industry. New employees are expected to spend their working lives with the firm, and regularly go through intensive training programs to upgrade their skills. "We hire with a career in mind," says Edward Krieg, directory of management development. Although some overseas IBM plants are unionized, the firm has never had a union vote in any U.S. facility.

From "The Colossus That Works," _Time_, 11 July, 1983, pp. 45-6. Reprinted with permission.

The generous fringe benefits extend to recreation. The company provides memberships for less than $5 a year in IBM country clubs in Poughkeepsie and Endicott, N.Y. There, employees can play golf, swim and participate in numerous other sports.

Watson was especially adept at motivating workers and inspiring loyalty. He personally commissioned a company songbook and led employee gatherings in numbers like "Ever Onward."* The song was belted out with gusto during get-togethers of the IBM 100% Club, made up of members who have met 100% of their sales goals for the previous year.

*Sample lyric: "Our products are known/ In every zone/ Our reputation sparkles like a gem/ We've fought our way through/ And new fields we're sure to conquer too/ For ever-onward IBM."

WORKSHEET: JAPAN'S ENERGY POLICY

I. Japan's Energy Demand

	1977	1985	1990	1995
*Demand	355.5	502.3	604.1	696.1

Change in
Demand   _____   _____   _____

Percentage increase in
demand from 1977 to 1995: $\dfrac{1995 - 1977}{1977}$ X 100 = _____

*millions of tons of oil equivalents

II. Japan's Long Term Energy Plan

		1977	1985	1990	1995	Percentage Change (1977 - 1995)
1.	Hydro	4.8%	4.7%	4.6%	4.6%	_____
2.	Geothermal	0.0%	0.4%	1.0%	1.8%	_____
3.	Domestic Oil & Natural Gas	0.9%	1.4%	1.4%	1.7%	_____
4.	Domestic Coal	3.2%	2.5%	2.0%	1.8%	_____
5.	Nuclear	2.0%	6.7%	10.9%	14.3%	_____
6.	Imported Coal	11.6%	13.6%	15.6%	16.5%	_____
7.	LNG	2.9%	7.2%	9.0%	8.7%	_____
8.	New Energy	0.1%	0.9%	5.5%	7.6%	_____
9.	Imported Oil	74.5%	62.9%	50.0%	43.1%	_____

© CTIR
University of Denver

III. Japanese Oil Imports in 1977
(By Country of Origin)
% of Total

Saudi Arabia *	30.1	
Iran *	16.0	
UAE *	14.7	
Indonesia *	13.8	
Kuwait *	8.2	
Iraq *	3.1	Percentage of Oil
Oman	2.6	Imports received from
China	2.6	OPEC members in 1977=
Neutral Zone	2.5	
Qatar *	1.5	_____
Other South East Asia	4.9	Percentage of Oil Imports
		received from non-OPEC
		members in 1977=
		_____

* Member of OPEC, the Organization of Petroleum Exporting Countries

MAP OF SOUTHEAST ASIA

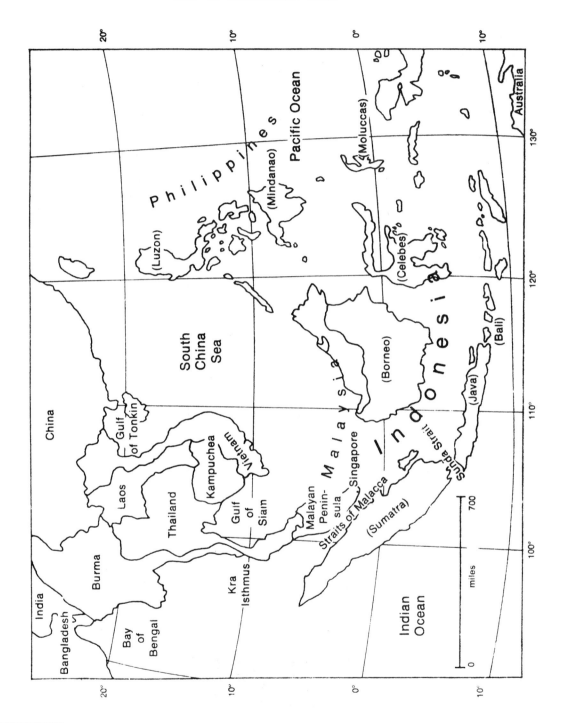

Map of Southeast Asia is from Intercom #89, Global Perspectives In Education, New York, NY, 1978. Reprinted by permission.

INDIAN DIVERSITY ACTIVITY SHEET

Part I: Locate the following on your map of India.

1. Ganges River

2. Brahmaputra River

3. Godavari River

4. Krishna River

5. Himalaya Mountains

6. Thar Desert (Great India Desert)

7. Deccan Plateau

8. West Ghats

9. Bay of Bengal

10. Indian Ocean

11. Calcutta

12. Delhi

13. Bombay

14. Madras

160

Part II: Using the atlases, answer the following questions.

1. During which season does one need a raincoat in India?

    _____

2. If you want to cross-country ski in India, at what time of the year would
    you go, and where would you go?

    _____

    _____

3. If you were to visit Madras what clothes would you bring?

    _____

4. What country is located south of India? _____

5. What country is located northeast of India? _____

6. Which geographic areas have a high density of population?

    _____

    _____

7. Why does Rajastan have a low density of population? (Hint: geographic
    reason.)

    _____

    _____

    _____

8. What is the capital of India? _____

9. The interior plateau _____ is separated from the lowlands by
    mountain ranges.

10. What are the "natural defenses" of India?

_____

_____

_____

11. Why have India's northern and northeastern borders become less secure?

_____

_____

_____

12. Does the diversity of geography/topography help or hinder development?
    List and explain three ways geography can influence the development of
    India.

_____

_____

_____

_____

_____

STUDENT ACTIVITY SHEET

Working as a team, complete the following:

1. Summarize the past political history of India from 327 B.C.--the invasion by Alexander the Great--to 1947 independence.

© CTIR
University of Denver

2. Briefly discuss how geographical diversity can help or hinder development. List and explain three ways geography could have influenced the development of India.

3. India has made many cultural contributions to the world. Some of them are represented in the answers to the following:

   A. List five of the religions of India.

      _____   _____

      _____   _____

      _____

   B. How has Indian philosophy influenced people in the United States? List several of the philosophies.

      _____   _____

      _____   _____

   C. List three world-famous architectures or works of art found in India:

      _____   _____

      _____

   D. Name two world-famous Indians (living or dead).

      _____   _____

4. Find the following information:

   Per Capita Income: _____

   Gross National Product: _____

   Major imports: _____

   Major exports: _____

   Population: _____

   Literacy Rate: _____

   Life Expectancy: _____

   Number of languages: _____

   Number of radios per 1000 people: _____

165

Number of TVs per 1000 people _____

Nuclear capability: _____

5. Using the data your team researched, do you believe that India is developed or underdeveloped? Give specific reasons for your opinion.

6. Look over all your answers to questions 1-4. Does India fit your group's criteria for development? Why or why not? Would you change any of your criteria? What factors do you think are most important to the development of a nation?

© CTIR
University of Denver

CIRCLE OF COMPLEXITY

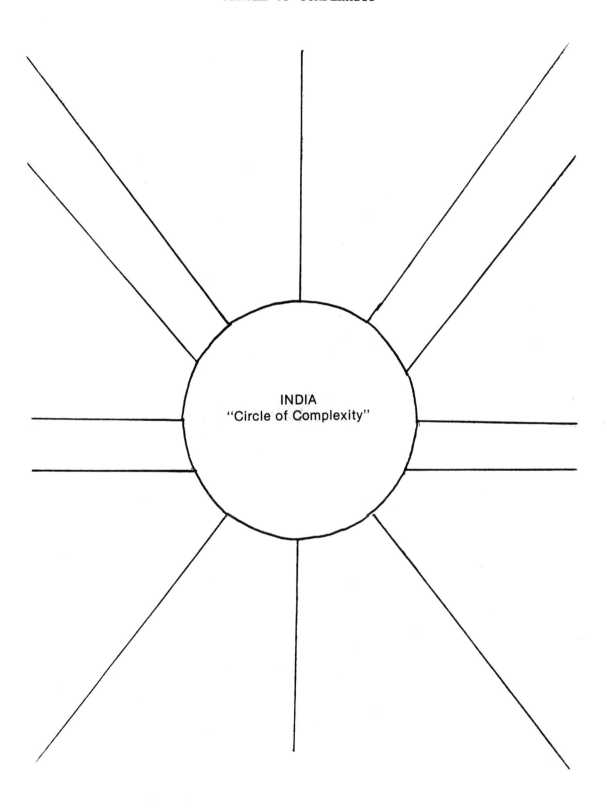

DATA SHEET

POPULATION: 762.2 million

BIRTH RATE PER 1000: 34

YEARS TO DOUBLE POPULATION: 32

POPULATION BY THE YEAR 2000: 990.6

TOTAL FERTILITY RATE: 5.3

PROJECTED ULTIMATE POPULATION SIZE: 1,642.8 (millions)

URBAN POPULATION: 23%

POPULATION UNDER AGE 15: 39%

POPULATION OVER AGE 64: 3%

LIFE EXPECTANCY: 53

POPULATION PER PHYSICIAN: 2,600

INFANT MORTALITY RATE: 118 (per 1,000)

DEATH RATE: 13 (per 1,000)

GROSS NATIONAL PRODUCT: 184,128 million

GNP PER CAPITA: $260.00

AVG. GROWTH RATE: 2.2%

ECONOMY: Industries: textiles, steel, processed foods, cement, machinery
          Crops: rice, grains, coffee, sugar cane, spices, tea
          Minerals: coal, mica, manganese, salt, iron

TRANSPORTATION: passenger cars, 769,200; commercial vehicles, 628,100; civil
                 air travel, 8,316 km

COMMUNICATIONS: television sets, 275,000; radios, 14.08 million; telephones,
                 2,247,187; newspapers in use, 16 per 1000

Source: 1985 World Population Data Sheet, Population Reference Bureau,
Washington, D.C. and World Military and Social Expenditure 1985. Ruth Leger
Sivard, World Priorities, Washington, D.C.

LANGUAGE: 15 recognized languages; Dravidians 25%; 1000 "mother tongues"

EDUCATION: 36% literacy

RELIGION: Hindus 84%; Moslem 10%; Christians 2.6%; Sikhs 1.9%; Buddhist 0.7%;
            Jains 0.5%

169

SEABED NO MONOPOLY OF RICH: GOKHALE

Union Law Minister H. R. Gokhale said here today India would unceasingly strive for achieving a convention on the law of the sea, which would lead to the establishment of a more balanced and just international economic order.

He was inaugurating a seminar on the recent development in the law of the sea organised by the Centre for Studies in International Law at the School of International Studies, Jawaharial Nehru University.

Mr Gokhale said the traditional international law had ignored the question of inequities and imbalances in the economic relations between States. With the emergence of more than 100 developing countries in the United Nations, it had been realized that durable peace could not be achieved without a sound international economic order.

He described the third United Nations Conference on the Law of the Sea in 1973 as the most important ever held in diplomatic history. The developing countries had utilized the historic opportunity for working towards a fair regime for the uses of the entire sea and the seabed for their uses as well.

They could move forward from the accepted norm of the freedom of the seas which assumed unbridled competition to the advantage of the advanced nations, he added.

Mr Gokhale said the Geneva Convention of 1958 was totally inadequate to cope with the radical change in the contemporary economic significance of the oceans and their resources.

The concepts of "exclusive economic zone" and "the common heritage of mankind" in relation to the international seabed area and its resources were some of the revolutionary and direct products of this conference in 1973, he said.

Mr Gokhale said the knowledge of the ocean and its resources was still partial, but everyone was aware that the oceans were rich in oil, gas, manganese nodules, salt, magnesium and a host of other items. Important fishing grounds were also located within 200 miles of the shore.

The minister said India was deeply interested in these new concepts with its 4,000-mile coastline and international channels of navigation passing "close to our chest." The importance of the exploitation of petroleum resources in India's continental margin could not, therefore, be overstated.

Reprinted from The Hindustan Times 12/4/76.

India, he said, was keen that the international seabed area did not become the monopoly of the technologically-advanced countries for various reasons. India's continental shelf was now a proved oil-bearing region and the country also had 1,280 islands and islets.

About half of this constituted the Archipelago of Daman and Nicobar Islands, on the one hand, and the Lakshadweep, on the other. India, therefore, had a vital interest in evolving an appropriate regime for archipelagos and islands.

Developing countries, Mr Gokhale said, did not share the view of the industrialized countries that the proposed international Seabed Authority should be a mere licensing body.

Their position was that international seabed area and its resources were the common heritage of mankind. All activities of exploration of the area and exploitation of its resources should be conducted directly by the authority through an enterprise to be established as an operational arm of the authority.

Within its discretion and to the extent considered necessary, the authority might associate States and private entities with exploitation activities. The developing countries had taken the position that they would not agree to the dual system of exploitation as proposed by the technologically-advanced countries. Developing countries should have the right to participate in all stages of exploitation activities and transfer of technology to them.

On pollution, he said, India and several developing countries had taken the position that while standards in regard to vessel based pollution could be international, the coastal State alone should have the competence to take enforcement action in the economic zone.

SATELLITES FOR GLOBAL OBSERVATION

ONE of the first uses of man-made satellites was for observing weather from space. Satellites are capable of surveillance over a large area of the earth and obtaining information immediately. Weather is global in nature, and satellites have provided an observing tool that is truly global and instantaneous.

Satellites generally observe weather by 'remote sensing' of the earth and its atmosphere. In simple words, remote sensing is observing an object with the help of sensors not in direct contact with it, for example, seeing a cloud with your eye. Remote sensing is done by sensing electromagnetic radiations from objects. These radiations include visible light rays as well as ultra violet rays, infra-red rays and microwaves (the radiowaves of very small wave-lengths like those used in radars and modern telecommunications). How this technique has been applied to weather observing is a fascinating story.

The first weather satellite. TIROS-1 (acronym for Television and Infra-Red Observational Satellite), was launched by the US on April 1, 1960. It transmitted to earth the first TV pictures of clouds which showed organisations of weather systems extending across thousands of kilometres of ocean and land areas with a clarity never seen before. Many storm systems would have remained undetected but for these pictures. Improvements in later satellites made it possible by 1965 to obtain daytime cloud cover pictures of the complete earth once every 24 hours. Soon, weather satellites were orbiting round the earth from pole to pole, and transmitting real time cloud pictures to anyone setting up a ground receiving station. In India six such direct readout stations, called Automatic Picture Taking or APT stations, have been established at Bombay, Calcutta, Gauhati, Madras, New Delhi and Pune. Satellite pictures received at these centres are used for weather analysis, forecasting and adverse weather warning.

TV cameras placed on the early satellites could take pictures of only the daytime portion of earth which was illuminated by sunlight. No pictures were transmitted by them at night. As against this all objects on earth and in the atmosphere emit infra-red rays at all times, depending upon their temperature and surface properties. An infra-red picture can be taken at any time of the day or night with the help of a sensor called "radiometer". By 1972, satellite TV cameras were replaced by such radiometers which transmitted day-and-night-time cloud pictures in real time and provided complete earth coverage twice a day. The present-day NOAA satellites of the US and METEOR of the USSR have similar sensors. NOAA satellites orbit round the earth once in 115 minutes at an altitude of about 1,500 km. Pictures taken by their Very High Resolution Radio-meter can detect any cloud or small-scale weather system of 1 km size.

Another kind of weather satellites are geostationary meteorological satellites. They are placed in orbit around the Equator at an altitude of 36,000 km above the earth's surface so that they complete one orbit in 24 hours—the same time as taken for one revolution of the earth. Such a satellite appears stationary relative to the earth's surface, and can undertake continuous surveillance of weather over more than one-fourth of the earth.

The US has been operating such weather satellites over the Atlantic and Pacific Oceans for the past 10 years. The present US satellites, called GOES (Geosynchronous Operational Environmental Satellite), provide a full earth view once every 20 minutes with a ground resolution of 900 metres. GOES can also be commanded to monitor a smaller earth area at more frequent intervals. It is a powerful tool for observing global weather systems, for deriving winds in the atmosphere, and for tracking severe weather phenomena like tropical cyclones, cloud bursts, tornadoes, squall lines, heavy rain and snow.

Realising their tremendous potential, internationally co-ordinated plans are being drawn up to teorological satellites in the next two years in order to cover almost the whole earth. They will form a global observing system under the World Weather Watch (WWW). The USSR is likely to place a satellite at longitude 70 deg. E over the Equator, which will provide coverage for Asia and for the Indian Ocean. The extensive data on clouds, winds, sea temperatures, and weather systems of various scales from these sources will help in a better understanding and predicting of the monsoon.

A remarkable application of satellite pictures has been in tracking tropical cyclones over the sea where no other means of their detection usually exist. Satellite pictures instantly give their location, intensity and information about their future development. A cyclone classification, developed on the basis of their appearance in satellite pictures, permits an accurate estimation of their maximum wind speeds as soon as they are observed. The satellite photograph of the Porbandar cyclone at its peak intensity on October 22, 1975, a few hours before it hit the Gujarat coast, vividly depicts the killer cyclone with its coiling bands of torrential rain and hurricane winds, and the central calm 'eye'. Another picture shows the advance of the monsoon over the country with dense overcast clouds covering the east Arabian Sea, the Bay of Bengal, and part of the mainland.

Infra-red pictures also provide global maps of sea surface temperatures. They help in locating areas of sea water upwelling which have an abundance of fish, and in mapping warm and cold ocean currents. This information is being utilised for economic exploitation of ocean wealth.

Another kind of infra-red and microwave radio-meters have recently been developed for deriving vertical distribution of temperature, water vapour and liquid water content in the atmosphere. Microwave radio-meters also sense soil moisture over the land, surface winds over sea areas, and fresh snow or old ice deposits over mountains. This information will be useful in oceanography and water management. Some of these sensors are under development, but they offer vast potentialities.

Satellite information is being increasingly utilised in the weather services for aviation, agriculture, water management, snow survey, industry, shipping, etc., and a number of new areas are opening up for future applications. The resulting improvement in the weather services will provide much greater economic benefits to society.

The Hindustan Times Weekly Sunday 2/6/77.

STUDENT ACTIVITY SHEET

Country	Classification of border	Stability
Pakistan	Subsequent	No
China		
Nepal		
Butan		
Bangladesh		
Burma		
Sri Lanka		

© CTIR
University of Denver

THE PATRIOT

The statements below were written by an Islamic leader who was revolting against what he considered injustices in his country.

"When a government does not perform its duty, it becomes oppressive. If it does perform its duty, not only is it not oppressive, it is cherished and honored by God. The duty of government, therefore, must be clarified in order for us to establish whether the present government is oppressive or not.

Reason and experience alike tell us that the governments now existing in the world were established at bayonet-point, by force. . . Their foundations are all rotten, being nothing but coercion and force. . . .

When you go into (the capital), you see all the cars and that deceptive exterior, but you haven't gone to the other side of (the city) to see what state that is in. They don't have any drinking water. They have to take their pitchers and climb up those hundred steps until they come to a water faucet, then fill their pitchers, and climb down again. Picture some poor woman in the middle of the biting winter climbing up and down those steps to fetch water for her children. . .

We want our women to attain the high rank of true humanity. Women must have a share in determining their destiny. (The present government) wanted to treat woman as a mere object, a possession, but (our religion) grants woman a say in all affairs just as it grants man a say. All the people of (our country), men and women alike, must repair the ruins that the previous regime has bequeathed to us; the hands of men alone will not suffice to accomplish this task. . ."

NOMADS SETTLING DOWN

Although Lawrence has long since faded from Arabia, his romantic visions of desert nomads live on. Many an armchair adventurer remains convinced that Bedouin tribesmen still trek the sands on their stately camels, pausing periodically to fold their tents silently or offer a sheep's eyeball to an honored guest. If such was ever the truth, it's mostly mirage by now. According to a survey by the University of Jordan, the modern Bedouin tribesman is far more likely to pilot a pickup truck, live in a concrete house and serve more mundane cuts of meat. "The glamour of the twentieth century has attracted them, and it has changed their lives forever, "says sociologist Kamel Abu Jaber, who directed the massive study of latter-day Bedouins.

Today's settled-down Bedouin life-style is most evident in Jordan, where about 150,000 of the tribesmen dwell; others are scattered through Saudi Arabia and other Mideast nations. Only 20,000 or so still roam the Jordanian badiyah, as they call the desert, a far cry from the 80,000 or more who lived there just two decades ago. Driven from the desert mainly by drought, the Bedouins have been encouraged by the government to relocate in new settlements like Sama, a village of mudbrick and concrete in Jordan's Sirhan Valley, near the Syrian border. There, most residents tend olive trees instead of livestock, and they travel in cars rather than caravans. "I learned the art of agriculture, and it has brought me a better life," says wealthy farmer Abu Turki, who ended his wanderings after army service exposed him to other cultures.

Village life is much easier than existence in the often brutal desert, where adults have a life expectancy of only 50 years and 15 per cent of the babies die before their first birthday. In the settlements, Bedouin children get an education they never received as nomads, and many of their parents prosper as well. In Sama, for example, Abu Turki was given 500 acres of government land that his family once defended against Syrian troops. "Fifteen years ago, I was living in a goat-hair tent," he recalls, surveying his late-model Mercedes, color television and giant refrigerator. "Today I live in a palace."

Old Ways: While the transition to the settlements has been relatively smooth, many of the tribal traditions remain. The villages are built like tent cities, with the most important members at the center, and even educated Bedouin women still do not take outside jobs; 90 per cent will marry and lead domestic lives. Indeed, for all their new prosperity, some Bedouins mourn the passing of old ways. "I miss the freedom, the feeling of self-reliance," admits Abu Turki. "I miss being able to pack up at anytime and go anywhere."

Those nomadic days are clearly numbered, however, according to demographers. Within fifteen years, they predict, the last Bedouin wanderers will, in fact, fold their tents and steal away from the badiyah forever. Even now, the remaining nomadic tribes are changing their ways. Out in the desert, families use powdered milk instead of relying solely on the goats. And a young woman says she does not want her daughters to carry on their faces the traditional beauty tattoos of the Bedouin. "This isn't needed anymore," she explains. "What my daughters need is education for when they leave this life."

LANGUAGE FAMILIES OF AFRICA

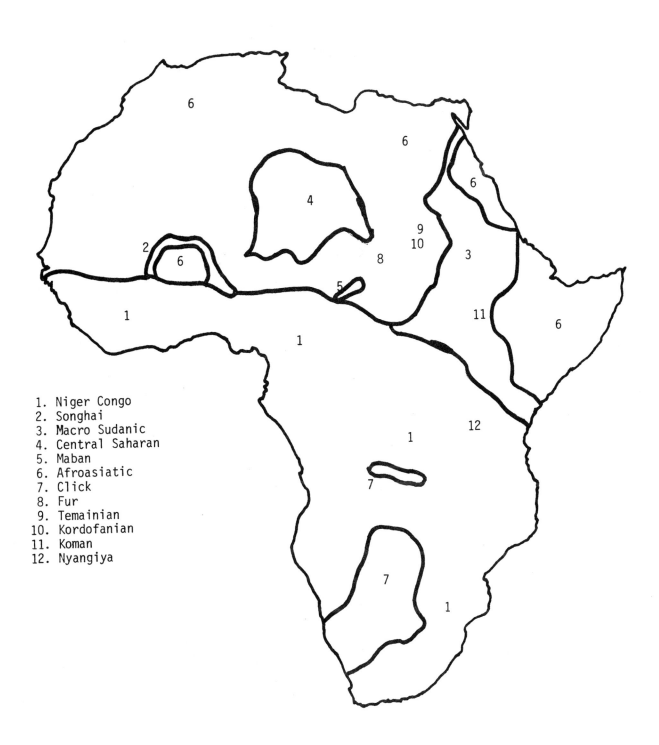

1. Niger Congo
2. Songhai
3. Macro Sudanic
4. Central Saharan
5. Maban
6. Afroasiatic
7. Click
8. Fur
9. Temainian
10. Kordofanian
11. Koman
12. Nyangiya

CULTURAL AREAS OF AFRICA

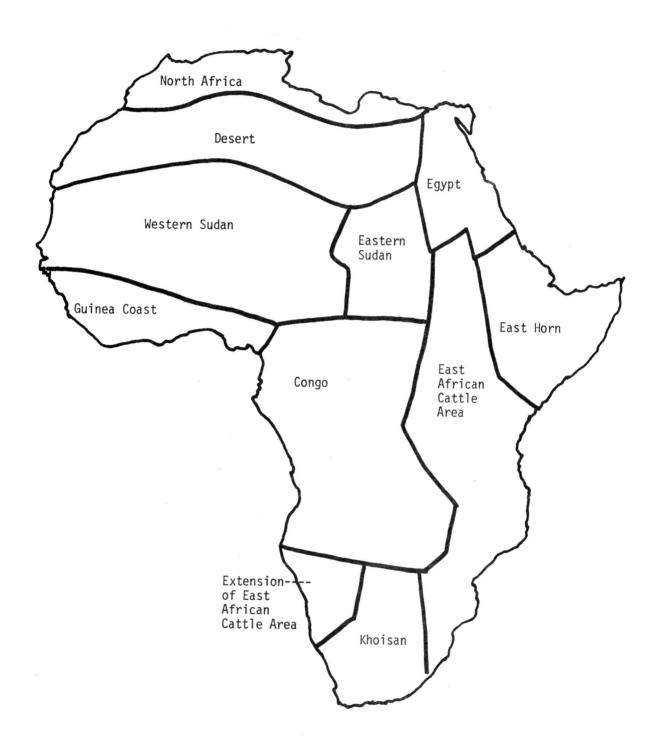

_____, THIS IS YOUR LIFE

This nation has an interesting and colorful history. Many explorers traveled through its wilderness, and colonizers used the paths opened by these explorers to build trade routes. Great Britain governed this colony through "indirect rule." Local leaders ran the day-to-day activities, while British officials carried out the monarch's policies. As with many ruled nations, the colony resented the British officials and their policies, so the colonists called for independence. The revolutionary movement was widespread, and it was encouraged by pamphleteers who wrote about the necessity for home rule. This colony eventually became an independent nation.

However, the problems were far from over. For many economic and social reasons, the northern and southern sections of this country could not get along. They distrusted each other. The North dominated the southern section, and the South decided to withdraw from the nation. This led to a bloody civil war, often called "the brother's war." The war greatly disturbed the nation's leader, and he worked to unite the North with the isolated southern section. The war ended after many men had died, but the country did emerge reunited.

This country's people represent many different cultures, and religious freedom is practiced. The official language is English. Today, this nation has the largest population of any country on its continent, and it is a major regional leader.

NIGERIA AND UNITED STATES: THIS IS YOUR LIFE

	NIGERIA	UNITED STATES
British colonialism	1861: Great Britain takes over the coastal city of Lagos. 1900: Nigeria becomes an official protectorate of Great Britain.	1607: The Virginia Company settles in Jamestown. 1763: The Treaty of Paris grants Britain the American interior east of the Mississippi.
Rise of nationalism	1930s: Herbert Macauley, "the father of Nigerian nationalism," writes in his own Lagos Daily News about the necessity of self-rule.	1776-1780s: Thomas Paine writes "Common Sense" and other pamphlets in Philadelphia, serving to ignite the revolution.
Independence	October 1, 1960: Nigeria achieves independence with a loose federation of states. October 1, 1963: the government creates a new constitution providing for a federal republic.	July 4, 1776: Declaration of Independence is signed. March 1, 1781: ratification of the Articles of Confederation. November 1789: the American states ratify the Constitution.
Civil War	May 30, 1967: Republic of Biafra secedes from the union signaling the beginning of a civil war. Union leader, General Yakubu "Jack" Gowon stated, "no victor, no vanquished." January 15, 1970: civil war ends. Gowon's successor General Murtala Ramat Mohammed is assassinated in 1976 because of growing distrust over his political moves.	December 20, 1860: South Carolina secedes from the union. February 4, 1861: seven southern states form the Confederacy, signaling the beginning of a civil war. Union leader President Abraham Lincoln stated, "With malice towards none and charity for all." April 9, 1865: Lee surrenders to Grant. Lincoln's successor, President Andrew Johnson, is nearly impeached in 1868 because of growing distrust over his political moves.

180

	NIGERIA	UNITED STATES
General Facts	Federal Capital: Abuja Population: 77 million	Federal Capital: Washington, D.C. Population: 222 million

NIGERIA'S ELECTION RETURNS SHAGARI TO POWER, BOLSTERS FRAGILE DEMOCRACY

The effect of Nigeria's closely watched presidential election, which returned incumbent Shehu Shagari to power for a second term, goes beyond its borders.

The Aug. 6 election was a crucial test for Nigeria's young and fragile democratic system. The peaceful vote in Africa's most populous state (now estimated with up to 130 million residents) is also seen as a triumph for democracy in Africa, which is dominated by single-party and military regimes.

President Shagari was elected to a second four-year term by a substantially larger majority than in the last election. The final results, announced early Thursday after four days of vote-counting, gave him 47 percent of the vote and a majority of more than 4 million over his main rival, Chief Obafemi Awolowo.

In the last elections, run by the military in 1979, voting was so close that Supreme Court arbitration was needed before President Shagari's victory was confirmed.

Early results had put Chief Awolowo in the lead, but these were from western Yoruba-speaking states where his support is strongest. Votes in the more numerically important but poorer northern states took longer to count and transmit to the capital, Lagos, in the south.

The north voted massively in favor of Shagari, a northern Muslim. The final result to be announced was from his northwest home state of Sokoto, where he won 91 percent of the vote.

President Shagari's victory reflected an ability to attract national support in a country divided by tribal and religious differences.

The country's Constitution requires that the President obtain 25 percent of the vote in at least 13 of the country's 19 states, as well as an overall majority. Shagari did so, and met his quota in 16 states.

The bespectacled President, who has the characteristic tall, lean features of the Fulani tribe, cuts an impressive figure in his long, white flowing robes. During his previous term in office, he developed a rare reputation for impartiality, moderation, and honesty.

Despite a much higher turnout--some 50 percent of the registered 65 million voters this year, compared to 35 percent in 1979--electoral violence and rigging have turned out to be much less than originally feared.

Peter Blackburn, Special to The Christian Science Monitor.

There seems to have been a unanimous reluctance by the six presidential candidates to repeat the thuggery and violence that marked elections in the early 1960s.

However, two of the candidates have initiated court cases, charging there was vote-rigging. Observers point out that such complaints are automatic in African elections. Even if the plaintiffs win, the overall result would remain the same, they say.

Officials in the National Party of Nigeria (NPN) hope that the President's resounding success will carry the party through to victory in the other elections this month -- races for state governorships and state assemblies as well as the national Senate and House of Representatives.

But the NPN's image is much less attractive than that of its President. The party itself is widely regarded as a corrupt and feudal elite. In the 1979 elections, it gained control of only seven of the 19 states.

This year all the main parties won at least one state.

State elections may be even more keenly contested than the presidential vote because under the country's federal system state legislators have a more direct impact on voters' daily lives.

NIGERIA'S NINETEEN STATES

F.C.T.-Federal
      Capital
      Territory

184

© CTIR
University of Denver

NIGERIAN PRESIDENTIAL ELECTION RESULTS

State	Total Votes Cast	Ibrahim GNPP % Votes Rec'd	Awolowo UPN % Votes Rec'd	Shagari NPN % Votes Rec'd	Kano PRP % Votes Rec'd	Azikiwe NPP % Votes Rec'd
Anambra	1,209,038	1.67	0.75	13.50	1.20	82.58
Bauchi	998,683	15.44	3.00	62.48	14.34	4.72
Bendel	669,511	1.23	53.21	36.19	0.73	8.60
Benue	538,379	7.89	2.57	76.39	1.35	11.71
Borno	710,968	54.04	3.35	34.71	6.52	1.35
Cross River	661,103	15.14	11.76	64.40	1.01	7.66
Gongola	639.138	34.09	21.67	35.52	4.34	4.35
Imo	1,153,355	3.00	0.64	8.80	0.89	86.67
Kaduna	1,382,712	13.80	6.68	43.12	31.66	4.72
Kano	1,220,763	1.54	1.23	19.94	76.41	0.91
Kwara	354,605	5.71	39.48	53.62	0.67	0.52
Lagos	828,414	0,48	82.30	7.18	0.47	9.57
Niger	383,147	16.50	3.69	74.88	3.99	1.11
Ogun	744,688	0.53	92.11	6.21	0.31	0.32
Ondo	1,369,547	0.26	94.51	4.19	0.18	0.86
Oyo	1,396,547	0.57	85.78	12.75	0.32	0.55
Plateau	548,405	6.82	5.29	34.73	3.98	49.17
Rivers	687,951	2.18	10.33	72.65	0.46	14.35
Sokoto	1,348,697	26.61	2.52	66.58	3.33	0.92
TOTAL	16,846,633	10.0%	29.2%	33.8%	10.3%	16.7%

185

A PRESIDENT FOR ALL SEASONS

ADVERTISER'S ANNOUNCEMENT

Federal Republic of
NIGERIA
ANNIVERSARY SPECIAL

A President for all seasons

President Shehu Shagari... he has stressed the need for a united effort in nation-building

NO one can write on the two years of Presidential Administration in Nigeria without dwelling on the character of the man at the pivot of the 'Shagari administration'. Alhaji Shehu Usman Aliyu Shagari was declared President after a historic election and was sworn in at an impressive ceremony in the famous Tafawa Balewa Square in Lagos on October 1, 1979.

Despite the bitter political wranglings that preceded his assumption of office, the 56 year-old President, in his inaugural address to the nation stretched a warm hand of friendship to the other four political parties in a genuine bid to establish an all-party government quite out of tradition with the presidential system of government.

The President said 'I urge all Nigerians to join me in working with resolution for the attainment of these goals. The first thing is for all those who have participated in the recent elections to work together whether they won or lost. Now that elections are over, we must act as good sportsmen, set aside differences and harness our energies to the task of nation building.'

On more than one occasion he even deemed it fit to call a meeting of leaders of the five political parties in order to discuss amicably the fate and fortunes of the nation and evolve mutually agreed solutions to the several problems plaguing the nation. At every step the gentleman President had thought fit to carry the entire nation with him through securing the concurrence of the leaders of the other four political parties with his programmes.

But at every step, the gentlemanly approach of the President was seen by some elements who are committed opponents of his programmes as well as the media under their control as either a sign of weakness or an admission of incapability to rule. This trend continued even after the President's party had agreed on a working accord with one of the other four political parties.

Yet, in the face of gross and egregious provocations by hostile media houses and the unpalatable effusions of their political masters, Alhaji Shehu Usman Aliyu Shagari continued to show restraint, to demonstrate the fact that the entire country is his constituency and that he is responsible — indeed, accountable — for the fate and fortunes of every part of the country.

Hence when in August, 1980, a flood disaster occured in a State in the country recognised as the citadel of opposition to his administration President Shagari did not only make an instant tour of inspection of the ravages of the flood but declared the area a disaster area and ordered the release of N3 million for the relief and rehabilitation of the affected families.

Such is the sterling quality of the President with which Nigeria has been blessed that in the Federal Republic of Nigeria many shudder to think of what would have happened to the Second Republic if Alhaji Shehu Shagari had not been elected President. ◼

Reprinted with permission from <u>Africa Journal</u>, October 1981, p. 93.

JUAN VERDAD: EDITOR

Juan Verdad is the editor of Barbarica's largest news magazine, Important Times. He is very concerned about the impact of domestic and foreign investment on the well-being of Barbarica's people. Wealthy foreign and Barbarican investors want to develop the mineral-rich land in the unexplored interior of the country. Juan discovered that members of the Indiqi tribe, who live on the land, are being threatened to get them off the land, and in some cases, tortured or murdered.

Juan published this story in his magazine revealing the atrocities. He hinted strongly that foreign and domestic investors, along with the national government, might be responsible.

The day after the story was published, Juan Verdad and two assistant editors from Important Times disappeared. The government denied knowledge of their whereabouts. Verdad's family and friends decide to look for him.

© CTIR
University of Denver

RULES AND GUIDELINES

1. <u>Your objective is to find Juan Verdad.</u> Remember: at times you must take chances in order to get information or to pressure the authorities. On the other hand, if you're in jail, you can't help to find Juan.

2. When the narrator reads the consequence of your choice, <u>react to the consequence</u> when the next set of options is read.

3. <u>Listen carefully to the story.</u> A case such as this is very complex; there are many actors and forces at work. Try to analyze people's actions as the story unfolds.

IMPORTANT ACTORS IN THE STORY

Juan Verdad, editor of <u>Important Times</u>

Jose Bolochet, President of Barbarica

Gerald Lewis, President of Supremia

James McPatrick, Supremian Ambassador to Barbarica

<u>Newtime</u>-a relatively conservative Supremian newsmagazine

<u>Supremia Herald</u>-a relatively liberal newspaper

Humongous International (HI), a Supremia-based multinational corporation with worldwide mining interests

Barbarican Council for Peace and Justice (BCPJ), an underground resistance movement

Indigi Tribe, poor native Barbaricans who live in the interior of the country

Amnesty International, an international organization devoted to curbing human rights abuses

ROLES

Juan's Mother: Your son has always been "into causes." You have spent most of your life worried for your son. Now, your worst fears have come true. Your son is gone, but his disappearance has put your whole family in jeopardy. You ask yourself at every decision: "should I risk my family to find Juan?"

Juan's Wife: You and Juan discussed the possibility of him being kidnapped or killed and the two of you decided that the rest of the family should not be sacrificed for him. You love him, you miss him, but you keep your conversation in mind with every decision you are asked to make.

Juan's Son(s): All your life you have wanted to be like your father. You have championed every cause your father has taken up, oftentimes in a more vocal and spirited manner. Now your father is gone, and you vow to find him at all costs.

Juan Daughter(s): Your father is a very important person in your life, but your fiance' is an important government official. Your wedding is next month, and you don't want it jeopardized. You want to find your father, of course, but you take no risks that would publicize the disappearance too much.

Juan's Sister: Your brother has always been involved in causes, and he has always brought hardship and fear to the family. You knew this was coming, and you can't understand why he would continue to risk the family for causes that will not benefit the family at all.

Juan's Brother(s): You want to find Juan, because he has always been a good brother and has always helped you out when you needed him. However, you have four children and a good job, so you consider these factors when you take any risk.

Indigi Social Worker(s): Juan has been an important ally in the fight for the Indigi cause against exploitation. You know that his disappearance is only the start of more suppression and hardship for the Indigis. You will use all your resources and take all risks to find Juan.

Priest(s) and Nun(s)   You have watched Juan champion many causes for all the impoverished people of Barbarica. His disappearance is a violation of freedom of speech, a basic human right, in your opinion. Therefore, you feel this should become an international incident, a calling card to all nations to fight political repression. You will take as many risks as needed to make this incident internationally known.

International Journalist: Juan Verdad's disappearance is a deathblow to your profession and all that newspapers stand for --the dissemination of objective information, the guarding of people's rights against the government, the right to have opinions. You will take as many risks as necessary to keep freedom of the press alive.

Domestic Journalist: Juan has been your editor, so his disappearance complicates your life enormously, for you are now the one to make decisions about Important Times: what stories to cover, what to run in the paper, and how to report on Juan's disappearance. You realize that one wrong move may cause your own disappearance.

Local Mayor: Juan's family and magazine have helped you maintain your political office throughout the years. On the day Mrs. Verdad came to ask for help, you were also visited by a government official who asked you to work with the authorities. He offered you an appointment in the federal government, so every decision you make must take into account your alliance with the Verdads as well as the benefits to your political career.

Underground Activist(s):   Although never actually meeting Juan Verdad, he has been a champion of all your causes, so you will take as many covert risks as possible to aid Juan, both in jail, and when he gets out.

"MISSING" NARRATIVE

Verdad's family and friends decide to look for him. First they go to his office at Important Times. There they learn from Verdad's coworkers that he kept a special file containing revealing documents about the Indigi massacres. Upon opening the file, they find that the papers are gone.

WHAT SHOULD YOU DO NEXT?

A. Write a letter to the Barbarican government pleading for information about Verdad.

B. Write a news story/letter to the editor or give an interview to a news agency accusing the government of causing the disappearance of Verdad and the other two men.

C. Do nothing and keep quiet.

D. Own choice

1

> For those choosing B: You are taken in by the police and interrogated. You are given a stern warning to avoid public action in these matters. International Journalist never goes to jail in any consequence.

One Underground Activist is placed in jail and never let out, is not able to communicate with anyone, and no information is available to anyone.

Verdad's friends and family decide to visit the Director of Public Information. They ask him if he knows anything about Verdad, but he only repeats the government's position -- that the national government has no knowledge of the disappearances.

WHAT SHOULD YOU DO NEXT?

A. Lead a demonstration in front of the Director of Public Information's Office.

B. Ask the Supremia Ambassador for help.

C. Go home and do nothing.

D. Own choice.

2

> For those choosing A: People involved in the demonstration are now missing. You are no longer part of the Verdad search.
>
> For those choosing B: You are picked up by the police, beaten, interrogated, and released. They warn you not to get involved.

The Domestic Journalist, Indigi Social Worker, and any underground activists are sent to jail.

The two assistant editors are released from the city prison. They tell Verdad's family and friends that the last time they saw Verdad, he was being taken to another jail, but that he was indeed alive. However, he needed help from the guards to walk. The assistant editors assume that Verdad has been tortured. They warn everybody that the government will not tolerate efforts to direct public attention to the Verdad disappearance. In addition, the Supremia Ambassador to Barbarica grants an interview to a reporter which is printed in Newstime, a Supremia magazine. Here is an excerpt from the article:

> James McPatrick, Supremia's Ambassador in Barbarica, expressed today in a phone interview that the Supremia government has "full and unabashed confidence in the integrity of Humongous International and the Barbarican government." He did not mention the mysterious disappearance of Juan Verdad, editor of Important Times, nor did he comment on accusations that Verdad is being tortured by the government.

WHAT SHOULD YOU DO NEXT?

A. Contact the Barbarican Council for Peace and Justice.

B. Go to the jail and demand to see Verdad.

C. Go home and lock the door (i.e., "do nothing")

> 3 If you choose A and are Priests or Nuns, you go to jail. For those Choosing B: You are locked up for 24 hours and beaten. You receive no food. The authorities do not charge you with anything, but warn you not to make any trouble. You are released and join Verdad's other friends who are contacting the BCPJ.

D. Own choice.

The leaders of the demonstration against the government are released and join Verdad's family and friends at an underground meeting. At the meeting, the people voice their fears about Verdad's well-being. They resolve to find him. Through a contact in the government, the Council members tell the lookers that the government's policy against the Indigi people has been stepped up. They decide to start a worldwide campaign to put pressure on the Barbarican government, so they contact Amnesty International. They hope that the pressure will force the government to release Verdad and to stop the Indigi slaughter.

WHAT SHOULD YOU DO NEXT?

A. Write a story/letter to the editor/provide information to a news agency/ denouncing the Supremia government for doing nothing about the human rights violations in Barbarica.

B. Organize a boycott of Humongous International products sold in Barbarica.

C. Wait for governmental response to Amnesty International pressure (i.e., "do nothing").

D. Own choice

4

> For those choosing A: You find your dog dead in the bushes near your home. A note is attached which says: "You're next." For those choosing B: You are picked up by the police and detained for 24 hours.

An important newspaper in Supremia, the Supremia Herald, prints Verdad's original story as well as an editorial accusing the Barbarican government of denying human rights, suggesting that Verdad's case may only be the tip of the iceberg. This causes a great sensation in Supremia, and the citizens there pressure their politicians to do something. The Supremia Ambassador responds to this pressure with the following news release:

> Embassy Press------(Dateline) BARBARICA
> The nations of Supremia and Barbarica have a long history
> of solid relations. It is unfortunate that certain
> elements in Supremia choose to undermine that relationship
> with unfounded accusations. I have the utmost confidence
> that if there has been any wrongdoing, of which at this
> date there is no evidence, it will be investigated
> thoroughly.

Meanwhile Amnesty International letters pour into the Barbarican President's office. Although Verdad's friends and family are encouraged by the international pressure, the government continues to deny knowledge of or responsibility for his absence. The government claims to have questioned some low-ranking officials, but Verdad's friends consider this as tokenism.

WHAT SHOULD YOU DO NEXT?

A. Organize a public demonstration in Barbarica's National Plaza.

B. Go visit the Director of Public Information again.

C. Do nothing. (Remind students they cannot "do nothing" twice in a row.)

D. Own Choice

5 | For those choosing A or B: You are arrested and thrown in jail.

The Barbarican mass arrests cause an uproar in the Supremian media. Ambassador McPatrick requests a private meeting with the Barbarican President, Jose Bolochet. The Supremia Herald prints an editorial speculating about the content of the meeting. (Pass out Handout #53 and read it out loud.)

The next day Verdad is pushed out of a speeding car, weary, but alive. He is stripped of his post as editor of Important Times, and the government takes over the magazine. (Let one-half of the jailed participants out of prison.)

© CTIR
University of Denver

SUPREMIA HERALD

Editorial: By the Foreign Journalist

President Bolochet must feel like a chastised little boy as he returns to the presidential mansion after his meeting with Ambassador McPatrick. Because Supremia pays for three-quarters of Barbarica's total foreign aid package, the threat of aid suspension was probably dangled in front of Bolochet as a very real and effective means of altering Barbarican policy.

Until now, Supremia has been content to let the Barbaricans solve their own problems. Why should President Gerlad Lewis' Administration suddenly care about a popular disturbance in a small country? In the first place, yesterday's mass arrests were no small "popular disturbance," but a clear violation of political rights. Further, President Lewis cares because the Supremian citizens care. The upcoming election, no doubt, has something to do with his increased responsiveness.

Bolochet has other powers to answer to than the Supremian Administration. Humongous International, a Supremia-based multinational corporation, is not known for investing in unstable countries. The recent disturbances in Barbarica make the corporate board very nervous. Bolochet need only recall HI's pullout from San Ruffia last year when labor riots in that nation destroyed many newly dug mine shafts.

Amidst all the power politics, though, we only hope that the pressure on the Barbarican government does some good and that Juan Verdad is found alive.

POWER PLAY: A CENTRAL AMERICAN DRAMA

In this play, you and your classmates will assume the role of people in a Central American country. You must decide together which country will be the setting and which of the following roles you would like represented:

Government officials
Church
Army
Guerrillas
Landowners
Indians
Peasants
Urban Poor
Women and children
Students
Middle class professionals (teachers, doctors, journalists)
Labor union leaders

Decide which groups represent the powerful and which represent the powerless. (Some groups such as the Catholic Church and women and children may be split between those who are powerful and those who are not.)

Research

Research the following questions from the point of view of your assigned role:

What are your most important sources of power?

To which other groups are you most closely allied?

What forms does this alliance take?

What strategies should your group use to deal with your opponents?

Historically, how has your group related to the power structure in your country? How has it related to opposing groups?

What is its position in the power structure today?

The Play

Your task is to write the script of a play, entitled "Power Play," which dramatizes a confrontation between the powerful and the powerless in your country. You must follow this general outline:

© CTIR
University of Denver

SCENE I: The powerless discuss their problems and what they can do about them.   (Script written by those groups designated powerless.)

SCENE II: The powerful discuss the sources of their power and their strategies for dealing with the powerless.   (Script written by those groups designated powerful.)

SCENE III: A confrontation takes place between the powerful and the powerless.   (Script written by a representative committee of both groups with all students allowed to improvise in their roles once the confrontation has been set up.)

SCENE IV: Conclusion (written by each student)   Include how you think the confrontation will end and what you think will happen to the power structure of the country by the year 1995.

© CTIR
University of Denver